The democratic process and the market

Changing Nature of Democracy

Note to the reader

The United Nations University Press series on the *Changing Nature of Democracy* addresses the debates and challenges that have arisen as "democratic" forms of governance have blossomed globally. The march of democracy has defined the close of the twentieth century; the fulfillment of individual and collective aspirations, good governance, and the nurturing of civil society form the benchmark of political organization. However, democracy defies a universal model, and the definition of democracy continues to be elusive. Moreover, the performance of democracy often fails to live up to its promise. This series explores two areas. Firstly examined is the theoretical discourse of democracy, such as the tension between procedure and substance, the dialectic between principles and institutions, the challenge of reconciliation and peace-building in democratic transition, the balance between universal and communitarian notions of democracy, between participation and efficiency, and between capital and welfare. Secondly, the series explores how these themes and others have been demonstrated, with varying effect, in a number of regional settings.

Titles currently available:

The Changing Nature of Democracy
The Democratic Process and the Market: Challenges of the Transition

The democratic process and the market: Challenges of the transition

Edited by Mihály Simai

United Nations University Press

TOKYO · NEW YORK · PARIS

United Nations University Press
The United Nations University, 53-70, Jingumae 5-chome, Shibuya-ku, Tokyo, 150-8925, Japan
Tel: +81-3-3499-2811   Fax: +81-3-3406-7345
E-mail: sales@hq.unu.edu
http://www.unu.edu

United Nations University Office in North America
2 United Nations Plaza, Room DC2-1462-70, New York, NY 10017, USA
Tel: +1-212-963-6387   Fax: +1-212-371-9454
E-mail: unuona@igc.apc.org

United Nations University Press is the publishing division of the United Nations University.

Cover design by Joyce C. Weston

Printed in the United States of America

UNUP-1026
ISBN 92-808-1026-x

Library of Congress Cataloging-in-Publication Data
The democratic process and the market: challenges of the transition/edited by Mihaly Simai.
    p.   cm.
  Includes bibliographical references (p.   ) and index.
  ISBN 928081026X (pbk.: perm. paper)
  1. Europe, Eastern-Economic conditions—1989–
2. Europe, Central-Economic conditions. 3. Former Soviet republics-Economic conditions. 4. Russia (Federation)—Economic conditions. 5. Europe, Eastern-Politics and government—1989– 6. Europe, Central-Politics and government. 7. Former Soviet republics-Politics and government. 8. Russia (Federation)—Politics and government. 9. Democracy-Europe, Eastern. 10. Democracy-Europe, Central. 11. Democracy-Former Soviet republics. 12. Democracy-Russia. I. Simai, Mihaly.
  HC244.D3735   1999
  330.947—dc21   99-6569
                                                   CIP

Contents

Case studies

Figures and tables

Introduction

Mihály Simai

The issues which are dealt with in this book have raised extensive interest and world-wide attention both in the academic community and in international political affairs, actively involving government, intergovernmental organizations, and NGOs. Dozens of books, hundreds of pamphlets have been written on the topics discussed here. Human history has witnessed different systemic transitions, but never before, at least during the period of modern history, have the challenges for these particular countries and simultaneously for the international community become so clear, due to the complex inter-actions between the past and the present, between the political, eco-nomic, and social processes, cultural values and institutions, national and international factors and institutions, as in the former socialist countries in Europe. The global information revolution, which has highlighted the transition process and its consequences, has added another dimension to the uniqueness of the changes.

This volume is a specific contribution to the global dialogue about the transition. It is as a part of the United Nations University's pro-gramme on the global democratic process and comprises one of the "regional" dimensions of it. The chapters focus on the historically more or less unparalleled changes in the former socialist countries, where democratization has not resulted from an organic process of

1

development, resting on other social and economic changes, but on "socio-political implosions," which included both internal processes (the collapse of the etatist-socialist regimes) and external factors (the dissolution and dismembering of the Soviet Union). The chapters, written by well-known specialists, mainly from the region, analyse the interrelations between political and economic change. The social transformation, the transition to a pluralistic democratic system of governance in the former socialist countries, has coincided with the construction of a modern market economy. Both of these processes are built "from above" and "from below" simultaneously.

The volume does not offer a thorough comparative country-by-country analysis. Certain countries have been selected which can be considered as having specific patterns, and some of the more general issues have been raised reflecting the main trends and tasks to be undertaken. The post-communist region is a diverse part of the world. There are great differences in the size of countries, in levels of economic development, social stratification, cultural background, language and religion, and in the capacity to deal with the complex tasks of building a democratic market economy. Furthermore, there are several unresolved ethnic, socio-political and territorial problems, which constantly threaten the region with crises and political disruption, and have the potential to create tensions and conflicts within and between countries. There is no simple and easy answer to such questions as to how strong or to what extent democracy is sustainable in this region.

Of course it is relevant to question the extent to which social scientists, only seven or eight years after the beginning of the transition, can draw firm, meaningful conclusions about the nature and sustainability of the region's evolving democracy and marketization. The tendency at the end of the 1990s may be to see the problems, constraints and opportunities more clearly, and conjecture only tentatively how the new institutions can handle the socio-economic conflicts arising during the transition from a centralized, totalitarian, non-market system to a modern, democratic market economy.

The Central and Eastern European (CEE) countries have been through three or four systemic changes in the twentieth century. Historically, these transitions were necessitated by political and economic breakdown or by serious limitations in the outgoing system. An important influence on the environment in which the achievements and the failures of different systems have been judged in the second half of the twentieth century has been exerted by external factors: the conflicts between the two antagonistic systems in the world. Political debate about systems during the Cold War were influenced less by the abstract model of socialism or the textbook model of the market system than by the shortcomings of "socialism" as it functioned in the Soviet Union and the CEE countries, and by the perceptions of the modern capitalist system as it developed in the industrial West. The latter projected a high standard of living in the developed industrial countries, their democratic systems, and their individual freedom and social welfare.

The issues raised in academic discourse on the performance of these systems have been broader and deeper than those raised in political debate, although the ideas espoused by various schools of political thought have had an important influence on them. Similar differences have emerged in the international debate on the transition.[1] Several Western economists, for example, tended initially to regard the transformation as a kind of ideological training ground on which to test their theories – radical, orthodox, gradualist, and evolutionist models alike. Others viewed the post-communist economies as a belated, delayed imitation of their own social and economic conditions. What they failed to consider was whether such neoclassical, market economic formulae and theses could apply to these countries without dealing first with the problem of how to establish capitalism, how to turn a command economy into a capitalist one.

Another dimension of the theoretical debates relates to an old dilemma. Which model of the market system should develop in the transition countries? Should it be one of the three main models – the welfare state, the liberal free market system, or the corporatist Japanese system – or should the former socialist countries take a "third" road? Will they develop hybrid, mixed economies, influenced by domestic and international pressures and processes? A significant, often controversial dimension of the debates relates to the social consequences of the changes, notably whether a rapid increase of inequality can be avoided, or whether it is a necessary outcome of the transition to the market system. Equality is the subject of a long-standing debate in the social sciences, of course, but in the context of the transition it has several specific aspects. A deep impression on people's thinking in the post-communist countries has been left by the *concepts of equality* embodied in socialism, encountered after centuries of feudalism or ethnic oppression. Public-opinion polls show that the vast majority of the population prefer the idea of equality to that of greater efficiency or rapid economic growth accompanied by social extremes and injustice. The issues of increasing inequality in the region have become a major *psychological* burden in societies where the calculable safety margins of normal living have been eroded. A key question for the future is the extent to which these societies will accept the responsibility and dignity offered to individuals by a democratic system as compensation for the vulnerability to which it exposes them.

The sustainability of democracy in the region became a basic issue in academic debate. It includes such questions as how strong and widespread is the loyalty to democratic values, particularly in the new political élite, whether the leading political forces are wise enough, and whether they can develop the necessary consensus in some fundamental areas indispensable to moderating and managing the conflicts inherent in the marketization process. Should the state play a greater role in regulating, limiting or stimulating market forces and their influence on societies, in a national or international framework? If so, who should do this and how should they deal with the ethical issues, the role of the welfare state, solidarity, global contracts, and so on? Explicitly or implicitly, many elements in these debates are reflected in the chapters of this volume. They deal not only with the practical problems of institution-building, marketization and reintegration into global markets, but with the theoretical aspects of the transition, the moral and ethical justification of the changes, historical comparisons with various other systemic transitions, and other, related questions.

The central issue is how countries are managing the main aspect of the changes in the region: the double or triple or more multiple task of making the transition from central planning to a market system, building a democratic system out of a totalitarian regime, reintegrating market economies into the global system and its institutions and building a new state on the ruins of the old structure. With the countries produced by the disintegration of the Soviet Union, Yugoslavia, or Czechoslovakia this additional task of building national institutions or even the nation itself is extremely complex. All these tasks must be achieved in a relatively short period of time. They have to be organized mainly from above, by a state, which has to restructure itself at the same time. One can characterize this complex process as "creative construction," by analogy with Schumpeter's concept of creative destruction. The elements of destruction are also present, since countries undergoing transition have to dismantle the institutions of the previous regime as well. The process is far from smooth.

Neither introduction of the market system nor democratization or reintegration into global markets is easy or free of conflict.

The book falls into two parts. The first deals with some of the general problems of the systemic changes and gives an overview of the interrelations between political change and economic transformation. The second part presents case studies of selected countries. Two of them – Hungary and Poland – are states that existed as separate political units before the systemic change. Four of them – Croatia, the Russian Federation, Slovakia, and Ukraine – are states that were parts of a greater political unit. The Russian Federation and Ukraine are the largest transition countries in area and population. The case studies do not follow an identical structure, because they are concerned with the specific characteristics and problems of their respective countries. However, they also reflect the many similar characteristics and problems, alongside the differences, in terms of the past and the present.

In principle, central planning offered a development process managed by the state as a solution to the twin problems of production growth and distribution. This was completely subordinate to a collective will ostensibly represented by the "visible hand" of the ruling party and its instrument, central government. However, the system failed to establish an efficient and competitive economy. The reasons for this failure cannot be understood in isolation from the external challenges and internal political factors and forces: the totalitarian bureaucratic state, the one-party system, and the politicization and bureaucratization of the economic processes. The need to reform the system was recognized at various stages in the Soviet Union and the other countries in the region. While some measures to change the functioning of the system were introduced in all these countries, the foundations were left unchanged. The most important and far-reaching reforms were the ones introduced in Hungary, as an indirect consequence of the 1956 revolution, but they too proved insufficient. The domestic structure of the regimes in the post-Stalin era, where direct forms of oppression and intimidation were replaced by less violent measures, were progressively undermined by internal conflicts, social, ideological, political, and ethnic. The CEE regimes in Central and Eastern Europe had sought to legitimize the political system by a promise of economic achievement and constant improvement in the standard of living. So their declining economic potential, external economic problems, growing indebtedness, and stagnating or deteriorating living standards (due to failures of economic performance) added new sources to the existing political conflicts. Popular uprisings took place in the region at a relatively early stage in the state-socialist period and were crushed by Soviet forces, at a time when the domestic political structure of the Soviet Union was still relatively stable. This internal political stability was gradually eroded as a result of the external and domestic political and economic failures, the long economic stagnation, and the declining standard of living. The policy of *perestroika* and *glasnost*, an attempt to change the character of the regime and replace the traditional rule of the party bureaucracy with certain democratic forms, tended to incite popular dissatisfaction. It also created serious conflicts within the ruling élite. Meanwhile ethnic conflicts emerged with great force. Gorbachev's policies also included ending the active and visible intervention in the CEE countries' internal affairs and changing the guidelines and limits for permissible change in the region. This encouraged not only communist reformers, but opposition groups intent on systemic changes.

The first chapter of Part I deals with the criteria and values for assessing the quality of economic systems.[2] This has hitherto been a neglected dimension in the debates about the CEE systemic changes. The author underlines that an economic system, whether a planned market or mixed economy, is not an autonomous sphere that can be the subject of detached and objective scientific enquiry, but a social construct. It reflects and influences the norms and values of a society, the aspirations of people, and obviously, the structures and *modus operandi* of power relationships. This means that a particular economic arrangement – a system, its positive and negative features and its overall quality – have to be assessed with social criteria, within a framework of political and moral philosophy. The main conclusion of the study is that the capacity of the market economic system to provide people with better living conditions amidst relative freedom is reasonably clear and difficult to challenge. None the less, recent developments in the developed market economies and the former communist and socialist countries are troubling. Everywhere from the United States to Russia and from the United Kingdom to Hungary, poverty and inequality have been increasing, sometimes dramatically. Could the main explanation be that the market economy is degenerating into market fundamentalism, upsetting the balance between labour and capital and causing an unbridled capitalism? Many governments have been abdicating their responsibilities and are becoming docile instruments of the "market," which is merely a convenient abstraction that masks highly specific interests. Elsewhere, the failure of the centrally planned economies was construed as evidence that "free" markets would suffice to ensure economic prosperity. "Reforms" were undertaken as if transferring assets from public to private hands were the alpha and omega of a good market economy. Experts and advisers from prestigious institutions gave an aura of technical soundness and legitimacy to policies that were often no more than crude expressions of greed and spoliation of collective goods and property. Conspicuous wealth, extreme poverty and despair, corruption, criminality, and widespread alienation are the natural concomitants. A market economy needs good, efficient government if it is to flourish and provide work and income to the maximum number of people. Unregulated markets without strong ethical codes simply give free rein to questionable human appetites.

The second chapter of Part I raises some important theoretical issues, by looking at historical and recent experience in the interactions between the democratic process and the markets, which have never been simple or straightforward.[3] The advance of democracy was a lengthy process in most developed industrial countries. It was influenced by social and economic interests and conflicts, political ideologies, ethnic problems, and external and internal factors and forces in each country. Democratic rights expanded progressively, often after bitter social and political conflict. Practically speaking, the spread of democracy followed in most cases from the growing prosperity of the people, containment of social conflict through reform, and increasing social mobility. The contradiction between a declared or constitutionally guaranteed equality of rich and poor and substantial inequalities in the distribution and redistribution of the national cake remained unmanageable while the cake was small. The capitalist system in very poor countries has not been able to sustain democracy without major setbacks. Capitalism and democracy in the second half of the twentieth century have coexisted well where there have been no major social tensions or conflicts, in a system that has been subjected to significant social reforms. Events in several European countries in the twentieth century have shown that a democratic system can be undermined by intolerance, ideological fundamentalism, violent nationalism, or internal or external events, forces and factors that create intolerable economic problems and unsustainable inequalities in society.

Analysing the process of the emergence of markets, the author states that there has been an interaction between the specific features of these societies and those of their markets. The former have created

7

the legal framework and set of organizations required for their markets to function properly. However, external factors have played an important part in market development and growth as well. Markets have played a multiple role in these countries, promoting an increase in the number of social groups and interests, and underpinning political diversity and pluralism. They have also promoted a concentration of economic power, and thereby a concentration of influence on the political power structure, and facilitated separation of the economy from politics. Markets have played a corrective role in cases of government failure. However, there have been market failures in many areas, necessitating corrective government intervention. All these developments point to the need to understand the historical environment in which the market and the political process interact. *The interactions become particularly complex when the progress of democracy and that of the market are mainly organized by the state, from above, rather than forming a generic historical process based on gradual change in society.* The author underlines that the relatively short time since the systemic changes and the differing speeds of economic and political progress and institution-building make it almost impossible to provide a detailed, credible, documented, comparative analysis of the interrelations between the economic changes and the development of democracy in the former socialist countries. However, a few general observations can be made: (i) there have often been different forces behind the processes in different countries, which in themselves have resulted more in divergence than convergence; (ii) in most cases, the two processes have taken place in parallel, and the interactions have mainly been indirect; (iii) the development of democracy has been influenced by the character of the regimes that preceded the change of system; (iv) the influence of external, international factors and forces has been important to the economic and political transformation, but the interactions of the two processes have seldom been surveyed in a systematic way.

The third chapter looks at the abilities of countries to deal with the evolving problems and the complexity of managing the transition process, and the role of the new neutral, professional civil service, whose establishment is essential for a successful, sustainable democratic state.[4] The author underlines that reform of bureaucracy in the former socialist countries forms part of the economic and political transition. Analysing the historical patterns in the transitions, the chapter differentiates between the organic and the functional character of the process. In the latter, which also characterizes the former socialist countries, the government and public administration have played a major part. Public administration everywhere, not just in the former socialist countries, faces many different pressures and challenges. Many people, for instance, are losing confidence in all kinds of public institutions, which themselves face pressures on their resources and budgets, because their existing commitments coincide with new demands. Meanwhile there are calls for more "direct" democracy and more opportunities for participation. These trends are accompanied by decreasing respect for the traditional instruments of "representative" democracy. In the CEE countries, the situation is even more complicated. The crucial issue is not to redesign, but to *establish* an independent, neutral civil service. This has to be done while democratization continues, far-reaching changes occur in the role of government, and the market economy establishes itself. So this civil service must be professionally expert and at the same time transparent and democratically accountable. Furthermore, the transition countries have several specific problems that present often difficult and unmanageable tasks to the system of public administration and its civil servants. Some relate to the diversity of the region, others to the transition process, particularly the widespread impoverishment and mass unemployment whose appearance has coincided with cuts in welfare services. These circumstances, coupled with the tasks of *institution and market-building*, place extraordinary pressure on the management and workforce in the public sector. There is also pressure to reduce public-sector spending, due to chronic deficits and calls from the general public for lower taxes and less official extravagance. On the other hand, the public is calling for more and better public services, while private-sector business wants to see an improved infrastructure and additional services to facilitate international competitiveness.

The state traditionally performs certain basic functions. The role of the state in the CEE countries increased in the twentieth century, with an accompanying growth of government bureaucracy as the etatist, state-socialist state took direct control over a wide area of economic and social activity. In some areas there is a degree of continuity, while in others there have been important changes in response to new requirements. A typical example of such continuity and change is the welfare function, including education, public health, pensions, social allowances, and housing. More important changes are taking place in the economic functions of the state, particularly in monetary and fiscal policy and redistributive objectives and instruments. Another important area includes regulatory activities to limit the adverse impact of behaviour: environmental protection, consumer protection, curbs on monopolies and cartels, and so on, where the importance of the state may be increasing. All these fields require major institutional and administrative reforms, and substantial changes in the role, composition, size, working methods, and quality of performance of the government bureaucracy.

The key elements of public-sector reform include privatization programmes, including contracting-out processes. Decentralization of decision-making to regional and local levels is required, to provide genuine legal and financial autonomy for local institutions. Also needed are deregulation and transparency, and transforming and flattening of public organizations, to make them proactive as well as reactive to match changes in public requirements and remands, and less expensive to run. Changes are needed in procurement policy, financial and human-resources management, and information systems in public organizations, so that government agencies can work more effectively towards new forms of cooperation with non-governmental organizations and the private sector, and give more attention to the citizens they serve. The performance and outcome of public-sector activities need to be measured by reviewing and monitoring, rather than commanding and controlling.

It is important for bureaucracies to maintain institutional stability and predictability while the changes continue. This presents major challenges for management and the staff of government agencies. Civil servants need new technical skills and new types of attitudes and values, but they must also preserve their traditional strengths. The specific examples in the chapter are taken from Hungary, where the process has been profound and far-reaching.

The author, in evaluating the achievements, states that it is difficult to say whether officials are more independent and neutral than they were at the beginning of the 1990s. The strategic objectives of the reform and the main trends in implementing it were unaffected by the change in the government's political complexion after the 1994 general election. Another positive sign has been the preservation of a distinction between political appointees in public administration and professional career staff. This means that growing importance is attached to independence, although the implementation process is slow in some respects. The delays are partly due to lack of expertise and a bureaucratic attitude, but partly to the complexity of the process. Another crucial issue raised by the author is whether the ongoing reforms should focus on greater autonomy, on business-like managerialism, or on the ethical requirements of day-to-day public administration. The author emphasizes that even in developed Western countries there is anxiety that giving the bureaucracy broader responsibility may threaten or weaken the legal state (*Rechtstaat*). The growing autonomy of bureaucrats and the expansion of business-like managerialism may damage the integrity of civil servants and the ethical foundations of the public sector. Obviously the danger of this and the ensuing damage will be greater in the CEE countries, where the legal state and constitutionalism lack strong historical traditions and political systems have generally been oppressive. The ethical damage has been very serious in the region because there was no legal transparency in public administration.

The case studies, which comprise the second part of the volume, cover specific problems that countries face in the process of building a democratic market economy. Of the Soviet successor states, the Russian Federation, including some other members of the Commonwealth of Independent States (CIS), and Ukraine have been selected, as the two largest countries, where the transformation has larger international consequences as well.

The political changes and economic transformation in the Russian Federation show many characteristics that differ from those of the CEE countries and of the other former Soviet republics.[5] Although there is a direct connection between political transformation and transition to a market economy, as in all the post-socialist states, Russia's position as a world power and as heir to most of the Soviet Union's economic potential, research capacity, and military might strongly influence the political process. As a result of the virtually bloodless "velvet" revolutions in the CEE countries, the collapse of the communist regime was followed by a new, still-changing system shaped by well-structured political forces. The impetus behind this anti-totalitarian, democratic transformation came from the reformist wings of the old ruling parties, the political dissidents and the anti-system opposition, with support from the general public. The forces of change were opposed to the command economy and in agreement about dismantling the party-state system. Society chose democracy, a constitutional state and respect for human rights, and has shown no signs of retreating from that choice. The social transformation in the former Soviet Union, and later in Russia, took different lines. The gradual evolution of the communist system effected during Gorbachev's *perestroika* was halted by the attempted coup by a conservative section of the communist leadership, and the subsequent dis-

11

solution of the communist party and disintegration of the Soviet Union.

The sheer size of Russia makes democratization and marketization relatively harder and more complex. Another factor is its ethnic diversity. Then there is the role of the Russian Federation within the CIS, the loose cooperation framework of Soviet successor states. Some CIS members look on Russia as an essential partner. Others, though willing to continue cooperation, feel menaced by the possibility that the "empire" may be restored. All these factors affect the interactions between the political and the economic factors and processes.

Gorbachev's slow, excessively cautious reforms, aimed at modernization rather than radical change, led to public discontent. The economic situation was visibly worsening and something had to be done about it urgently. The public expected the Russian leaders who had shaken off the tutelage of the party centre to take immediate, resolute steps to reform the economy on market principles. Added to that, there was the triumphant euphoria of the democratic forces after the defeat of the coup attempt, which aroused false hopes that radical reforms would bring rapid success. This explains why "shock therapy" was chosen. Furthermore, the policies of President Yeltsin were inclined towards short-term measures coupled with the use of force. The author emphasizes that Russia had traditionally strong etatist leanings even before the October Revolution. At the end of the 1990s there are diametrically opposite views about the role the state should play in the transition to a market economy. The opponents of shock therapy and monetarism accuse the government and state of being weak, of not using their authority, of being helpless in the fight against crime, and of failing to provide the institutional conditions for introducing an efficient market system. The main argument is that the Russian state is financially insolvent and weakened by corruption and crime. The Russian president, like the opposition, has called for law and order within the state, urging it to be healthier and stronger, and to exert greater control over economic processes.

Others accuse the Russian state of excessive intervention. Business people in various sectors, private entrepreneurs, and heads of enterprises and local authorities wax indignant about the way the state stifles production and business activity with taxes and bureaucratic interference. This further encourages fraud and tax evasion. Both these views contain some truth.

The Russian state has used its power mainly to distribute state-owned assets, instead of helping to build up the market, establishing efficient institutions, creating a competitive atmosphere, and ensuring strict compliance with market rules. Instead of reforming the system of public finance, it extorts taxes from the public and enterprises to replenish the depleted state coffers. In short, where there is a need for effective change, the state displays weakness, and where there is no need for such change, it tries to show its power. Unless the state regulates the market economy and intervenes in its formation, to provide the requisite social orientation, Russia and the other CIS countries will develop the kind of wild, robber-baron capitalism typical of Europe in the seventeenth and eighteenth centuries.

The situation is extremely diverse in the other CIS countries. Democratization of their political systems in the post-Soviet area has been impeded by their totalitarian past to a greater extent than has been the case in the CEE countries. The multi-tiered political system collapsed when the Soviet Union fell apart. Independence for the former Soviet republics meant that one political tier – the imperial centre – had been removed, which brought important domestic changes as well. The end of the party-state system "nationalized" and in many ways simplified the structure of political power and administration. However, an essentially authoritarian system of power has remained, even though formal institutions of democracy were established: a multi-party system, national presidential and parliamentary elections, and greater freedom of expression. Executive power in the Central Asian states and in Kazakhstan, Belarus, and Moldova is held by groups drawn from the upper and middle layers of the *nomenclature*. Most CIS countries are presidential republics. Some presidents have acquired the post for life or for a long term, through a referendum, and they have extensive powers, especially in Turkmenistan, Uzbekistan, Azerbaijan, and Kazakhstan. Often the presidency was obtained by the former first secretary of the republic's communist party. The old state institutions have been retained, including the militia and state security, and they are in an even more bureaucratic and corrupt state than before. The legislature is weak and rudimentary, and subordinate to or manipulated by the executive. The media are controlled by the executive as well, or else by an industrial and financial oligarchy. These arrangements have made it easier to maintain law and order and regulate the course of market reforms. But they have also placed obstacles in their path, by hampering the emergence of new policies and a market mentality.

According to the author, the heightened sense of national identity and delight at gaining state independence and sovereignty have helped to maintain political stability and led to some consolidation of society in the CIS countries. Most of the public considers it will be easier to attain economic and social progress within the framework of one's own state and this has ensured the top national political élite a credit of trust. The author emphasizes that in the CIS region as a whole, market freedom, without a state presence, law and order, and self-restraint by society's members, leads to savagery and chaos and a threat of degradation to the country. It is opening the way for manipulation of democracy and the market mechanism. On the basis of this chapter, one can raise a number of important questions about the future. Is it too early for example to proclaim the democratization irreversible in this region? Are the economic meltdowns the causes or the consequences of the difficulties of sustaining and consolidating democratic institutions? How will the successor states of the Soviet Union define their future path? At this point it is still too early to find a definitive answer to those questions.

The author of the chapter on Ukraine starts from the country's specific nature.[6] Ukraine is the second largest successor state to the Soviet Union. The transition to a democratic, market economy has also been affected by its ethnic diversity, its religious division, its inherited level of economic development and its structural deficiencies. Another important specific factor is that the transition coincides with the building of a political and economic infrastructure for independent statehood. Although the country had several national institutions while it was a member of the Soviet Union, these had limited powers and responsibilities. All these factors are complicating the changes and making them slower and harder than initially expected. Progress toward a new model for a democratic, market economy, based on respect for human rights and on economic prosperity, has been modest and faulting. Ukraine at the end of the 1990s remains in a deep political, economic, and social crisis. This background makes the interactions between democratization and economic reforms complex, controversial, and problematic. Ukrainian politicians and economists tend to view the market economy, social policy, and the process of democratization as three distinct areas. This favours authoritarianism rather than democracy. The Ukrainian political system does not fit into either of the traditional schemes, democracy or authoritarianism, so that there is constant, fairly tense struggle between them. The specific source of this process is a confrontation within the power structure itself – a struggle for access to the main instruments of power and for control over property. The participants of this struggle include various already consolidated financial and venture-capital groups, the agrarian lobby, the military industrial complex, regional clans, and so on. The gap between these and the general public is growing dangerously wide. The existing institutions do not do enough to facilitate active participation of the people in the political process.

A very interesting conclusion of the author is far from being pessimistic, however. Strange though it may sound, he sees the apathy and fragmentation of Ukrainian society becoming an important driving force for stability. The Ukrainian people – not forgetting the tough lessons of their long and dramatic history – are learning to rely on themselves and move ahead towards a stable future.

The problems raised in the other two case studies, on Croatia and Slovakia, are similar in some respects. Both countries are relatively small and both came into existence as the result of the separation from larger state structures.

In Croatia,[7] the political side of the transition began in the spring of 1990, with the first multi-party elections. Many other aspects of this social transformation were soon to emerge, some quite unexpected and tragic. Croatia faced, apart from democratization and economic transition, the huge challenges of building a nation-state after the socialist Yugoslav federation disintegrated, and of defending itself against domestic insurgence and outside aggression. Any one of the several problems the country faced at once would have sufficed in itself to occupy a generation. All the country's transition policies, political, social, and economic, have undoubtedly been influenced profoundly by the Yugoslav war and its aftermath.

Croatia's transition agenda covers more than a simple process of democratization. The author of the chapter highlights some of these agenda items, with special emphasis on the privatization process. (Market forces were already strong within the framework of the old Yugoslav state.) His working hypothesis is that the war dominated not only the political issues but the main aspects of privatization policy. The effort to defend the country from aggression (particularly after 1991) limited and directed the institutional choices and policy options. Developing and defending the state became the ultimate criterion in national decision-making. Only in an independent state could democracy and capitalism be realized. These priorities were configured "internally" by the dominant political ideology of the new ruling party, the political concepts of its leaders and the prevailing social and cultural values.

The author, in looking at the "post-communist" problems, under-lines the redistributive items. He states that redistributive policies involve a high level of conflict, a large part of the population (often the entire population), big changes in the distribution of social resources and power, and long time-frames. The radical policies announced by the new government after the electoral defeat of the communists indeed concerned large numbers of people and major social groups, and contained an inherently high potential for con-flict. They included denationalization and privatization, integration of Croats from abroad, redefinition of Croatia's position within the Yugoslav Federation, spiritual renewal and a return to cultural tradi-tions, a new state administration, and changes in the national struc-ture of state agencies (the police and army). At the same time, these were identification decisions concerning the state, its citizens, and the political, economic, and social system. The decisions on these redis-tributive issues had to be taken quickly, in most cases during the new governing party's first term of office. The only indisputable asset the new government possessed was electoral victory, which was generally seen as conferring legitimacy on the transition. The social and eco-nomic environment did not change much in the first couple of years. Although the political hegemony of the communists had ceased, many aspects of the communist period persisted. The economic sys-tem, the social structure and political culture, the weakness of civil society, the apparatus of state, and even the communists themselves remained. The political scene was additionally burdened with the processes of disintegration of the Yugoslav Federation, and the first indications of armed Serbian opposition to the new government. This developed in less than a year into fully fledged aggression, with war on land, in the air, and at sea. There was also a state of flux inter-nationally. Western governments and the various international agencies, baffled by the magnitude, speed, and quality of the changes, failed to respond to the rapidly developing crisis in the Yugoslav region. There was no political initiative or appropriate military re-sources forthcoming to prevent or contain the escalation of the war in Croatia, and later Bosnia-Herzegovina. The economic issues, partic-ularly the consequences of privatization, are increasingly returning to the agenda of the transition in Croatia. The author concludes that the legitimacy of the transition depends closely on the performance of the privatized economy. Members of the political élite are slowly realiz-ing the political cost of the economic transition. Blind to the social consequences of "wild capitalism," they counted on other sources of popularity and electoral support (war and the dangers to the integrity of the state). It is now clear that exposing citizens to the cold winds of the market while reducing their social protection evokes new problems that require greater attention from the government.

The other new state, the Slovak Republic, came into existence on 1 January 1993, through a division conducted in a constitutional and politically civilized fashion.[8] However, the split had several detrimental effects on the Slovak economy. This was the first time that Slovakia had existed as an independent state, apart from a brief period of limited independence during the Second World War. Slovakia is undergoing a process of search for its identity as a state. The author explains how Slovakia's historical position defines or affects various aspects of its development. Politically and economically, before the 1998 elections, there have been strong tendencies towards authoritarianism, attributable to the past political culture of a new state and to the fall in living standards and social security experienced by some sections of the population. These authoritarian tendencies increased the power of the executive branches and reduced the power and the role of the legislative and judicial branches of government. Also central to the country's concurrent processes of identification and integration has been the question of minority rights, which proved to be an essential factor in democratic transformation domestically and in international relations, including Slovakia's integration into the European structures.

The political process was also influenced particularly during the first four years by the gradual separation of Slovakia from the Czech Republic. Slovakia after 1993 had to define an economic strategy of its own, carefully considering the country's specific features. The separation was followed by a period of stabilization that prevented devaluation and inflation and protected the requirements for economic growth. This was partly due to the restrictive policies pursued by the central bank, the National Bank of Slovakia. Another key move was the introduction of import and exchange charges. These influenced the trends in the balance of trade and payments and increased the competitiveness of Slovak exports, which began to be reoriented towards the markets of developed countries. The chapter gives an interesting analysis of the interaction between the economic and political changes, and of the separate development in the two main areas of the country's life. The author states that by 1997, the Slovak Republic had successfully completed the introductory, stabilization period in its transformation process. So the focus shifted from the macroeconomic to the microeconomic plane, as the economy passes through an intensive process of restructuring, due to declining performance and competitiveness. An important conclusion of the chapter is that synchronizing the processes of nation-building with democratization and market development sets an extremely difficult set of tasks. Accomplishment of them requires a systemic approach, with constant analysis of the emerging political, economic, and social problems and tensions, to facilitate the identification of appropriate corrective measures and changes. The elections in 1998 opened a new, more favourable opportunity for implementing those corrections.

The two other countries dealt with in this book, Hungary and Poland, had some historical democratic traditions, relatively more liberal socialist regimes that admitted certain elements of a market system, and also greater exposure to the Western economic and political influence before the systemic changes. The political transition there took the form of a compromise between the old (communist) and the incoming political élite over the dismantling of the one-party state.

Hungary is one of the few countries in the region where the evolving conflicts between the economic and political transformation are the smallest and so far they have proved to be manageable. The chapter dealing with the transition in Hungary[9] explains this by reference to certain democratic traditions and the more recent developments during the more liberal socialist regime. Although Hungary during its modern history usually possessed institutions incorporating some elements of democracy, it was not a democratic country in the traditional sense. Establishment of a modern, democratic political system after the end of socialist rule was a radical alteration, but not an unprecedented one in Hungarian history. The return to a multi-party system recalled, for instance, the post-war political structure in the second half of the 1940s, and in some respects the political milieu of the inter-war period. So one cannot ignore the country's *traditions*, experience, and political cultivation when exploring, for instance, how far the new political system can handle society's conflicts and resolve its economic and social problems democratically, or whether the transition may produce conditions that jeopardize consolidation of the democratic system. The fact that the political transition itself rested on a constitutional basis was an extremely important asset. The Hungarian legislature amended the Constitution in 1989 and shaped the change of political system, based on a consensus between the ruling-party élite, represented by the government, and the emerging elite of the opposition parties. Since then, these legal norms have been legitimized politically by three general elections and by the rulings of the Constitutional Court. In spite of these favourable political conditions, a number of new problems developed in the political system. At the very early stage of the transition, the problems were mainly rooted in the interpretation of the liberal ideas and practices. There was no real assessment made of how the real model of liberal representative democracy functions in the developed countries. An assessment of the situation and political culture of Hungarian society was also lacking. There were positive and negative, subjective and institutional factors shaping the political culture. Of the institutional components, the author singles out the traditions of Hungarian parliamentarianism, where the two chambers were part of history. The ongoing debate in Hungary about whether a second chamber is necessary reflects a fairly wide spectrum of views about the need to broaden representation. There are, of course, those with opposing views, who are afraid that a second chamber would slow down or even block the changes necessary for the modernization process. On the other hand, the evolving problems in the functioning of the Hungarian parliamentary system bear an increasing resemblance to those in Western democracies. Conversely, many of the Western criticisms of the weaknesses of parliamentary democracies are increasingly relevant to Hungary, particularly the question of the limitations placed on real representation by the political parties, the conflicts between party interests and national interests, and the need for greater institutional participation by local authorities and civic groups in national decision-making.

The chapter also shows that the adverse consequences of the dual tasks of the transition – democratization and market-building – are largely responsible for the institutional and political problems: the mounting inequalities, the ways in which the privatization process was accomplished, the growth of poverty, and the changes necessary for Hungary's accession to the EU. The management and the solutions to these problems require further institutional reforms and a policy consensus whose establishment has proved very difficult in competitive political systems. The author mentions another important postulate that is missing from the region: a long-term vision of the trends of social development, to provide a better framework for policies and actions.

The transition processes in Hungary and Poland resemble each other in several ways. In both countries the process has reached a stage where the economic and political spheres have become to a large extent autonomous. Political tremors and battles have only a slight impact on the economy, whose development is driven by the market. The democratic system has gained solid institutional foundations, although there is still weakness in the underlying consciousness and culture of society, where ambivalent attitudes prevail. Freedom is universally cherished as an inherent value, but there remains a strong current of etatist sympathy and expectation of official intervention whenever difficulties are encountered.

While the chapter on Hungary emphasizes the political process and the institutional changes, the chapter on the Polish transition focuses more on the changes in economics, economic policies, and social structures, and looks at the interrelations between the economic and the social and cultural changes in a very specific way.[10] Traditions, of course, were also important in Poland. There were many features specific to the country. From an institutional point of view, there has been a democratic breakthrough, but democratization is far from complete and threats to democracy loom large. This is due partly to a paucity of democratic traditions and customs. Poland, historically, lacks experience of modern democratic statehood. The "gentry-democracy" for which it was celebrated in the fifteenth to eighteenth centuries was limited to a single class, and in any case degenerated rapidly into an anarchic oligarchy. After the partitions, the country's main regions came under the rule of the Romanov Tsars, a relic of absolutism by the mid-nineteenth century. The independence restored in 1918 began with a none-too-successful, short-lived experiment with parliamentary democracy, ended by a military coup by Józef Pilsudski, who introduced a mild dictatorship. After the war came 45 years of dictatorial, single-party, and for a period totalitarian rule by the communist party. A strong legacy of this whole experience is a tendency to see politics in terms of warfare, of unrelenting confrontation with opponents, while freedom is associated with anarchy. Although the pivotal moment in the change of system was the "grand compromise" at the 1989 Round Table, this did not perpetuate a belief in compromise as a civilized way of resolving political conflicts and rivalries. According to the author, Poland is nearing the end of the first stage of transition, having laid the groundwork for the new system and carried out the fundamental reforms by "shock-treatment" methods. The ownership and market reforms have gained the economy a considerable degree of independence from politics.

This does not mean that the main problems of the transition process or of economic and cultural modernization are over. That is far from the case, especially in terms of popular perceptions and acceptance of the new system. The difficulties there are greater than in the economy itself. Attitudes, as it were, have lagged behind the progress with economic reform.

The chapter offers a detailed analysis of the changing social structure of the population, the peculiarities of the middle class, and the socio-political consequences of the changes. An important specific feature of the transition in this respect is the large farming population and its political weight. Most of the farmers are smallholders, and they still account for 25 per cent of the population. They are the only example in the region of a large class of private owners surviving the socialist period and preserving their sense of a distinct identity. Poland's farmers were quick to organize politically and their party occupies a key position in the government. However, the attitude of the farmers to transition is ambivalent. Their economic situation and traditions place them within the free-market system, but their short-term interests and advantages prompt them to resist neo-liberal economic policies. There is wide support in the farming community for things like government intervention, protectionist tariff barriers, guaranteed prices for farm produce, and cheap, subsidized credits. So Poland's biggest group of private owners stands firmly behind many of the arrangements and institutions of the command economy. This is not as baffling as it might seem. Although the command economy did not eliminate peasant farming, it halted its free-market evolution. Above all, it arrested the process of land concentration, which perpetuated small, less efficient farms. While subordinating farmers to the state and making them dependent on government contracts, subsidies and allocations, the command economy also gave them a sense of security. It eliminated the competition and curbed the stratification among them. This resulted in a strong sense of peasant solidarity, so that even the owners of large, modern farms think in terms of a common class interest: they are still peasants rather than capitalists. Although changes in this mentality can be discerned, they remain slow, because Polish agriculture is backward, technically and economically, and incapable of withstanding competition from Western European farming. So the immediate interests of Polish farmers make them hostile to an open economy. Such a narrowly class-oriented, self-centred posture effectively conflicts with the interests of other major groups in society, especially urban workers. This is a Polish peculiarity. Meanwhile there has been a split in the working class, or more broadly, urban employees. The more active, enterprising, and on the whole more skilled members have moved into private-sector employment, where they can earn more, although they lose some welfare provisions. About a half of the blue and white-collar workers remain employed in the state sector of industry, which is plagued by considerable financial problems. Pay there is lower and the future uncertain, but the range of welfare benefits remains wide, although shrinking. However, the sheer size of this workforce gives it a sense of power and the leverage to exert effective pressure, which has significantly affected the way the trade unions' policies have evolved.

Another interesting similarity between Hungary and Poland is that the threats to democracy have more or less the same sources, the populist and etatist groups in the society.

The last chapter takes a more theoretical approach to the future of the democratization process in the region.[11] The author raises an important future dilemma, in this region and elsewhere:

There are various kinds of democracies, in space and in time. The traditional French version of democracy differs from the English one, and both differ from the American tradition, analysed initially by de Tocqueville. The democracy of the last century differs strongly from democracy in the first half of this century, which in turn differs from the democracy of the decades since the Second World War ... Robert Dahl aptly described the present phase as polyarchy. It is the highest stage so far in the development of the political system of human society, but it is not the final stage of democracy as such. It is a well-organized type of representative democracy, marked by a multi-party political system, in which parliamentary and municipal elections take place every four or five years.

Looking at the patterns of existing democracies, the chapter contrasts the possible choice between a "welfare state," "corporate democracy," and "'open' representative democracy," as potential alternatives for the region, which the author argues is at a critical stage. The situation offers the Eastern and Central European countries a special, historic opportunity. There have often been occasions in history, at the beginning of a new epoch and a new, developing system of relations, when countries neither in the first line nor very far behind it, neither part of the centre nor on the periphery, played a decisive role in forming the future. (That happened, for instance, to the United States during the nineteenth century.) The reason is clear. Catching up can offer the chance to create something new, and if the circumstances are right, this may be less difficult than transforming structures deeply rooted in the past. None the less, the author's conclusion is rather pessimistic:

The countries of East-Central Europe seem for the time being not to be able to take advantage of this situation, because of the difficulties rooted in the dual tasks of the transition, the consequences of the ethnic division of the region, the weakness of the institutional and political capabilities to manage the evolving problems in an ethically acceptable way, and to a certain extent because of the traditional and new sources of nationalism in the region.

The most important message of this book is that most former socialist countries have made appreciable progress towards a democratic market system in less than a decade. They have achieved more in this respect than many Western countries did over several decades of earlier development. They have created numerous political and economic institutions and conducted a redistribution of income and wealth that corresponds with a market system. However, there are important differences between them both in their achievements in building sustainable and efficient democratic institutions, in their degree of liberalization and the functioning of their markets, and in the internal distribution of the cost-benefits of the transition. Europe's former socialist countries have failed so far to establish conditions that promote a more equitable distribution of the inevitable human costs of the transition process. The majority of the population has suffered heavy economic losses. Unemployment and poverty are widespread in almost all these countries. Social diseases attributable to the transition process have led to a decline in human solidarity, compassion, and courtesy, and a deterioration in human relationships, including family ties. Indifference, egotism, cynicism, dishonesty, vandalism, delinquency, drug abuse, pornography, corruption, crime, and violence are increasing. The negative social trends are fuelling a popular desire for "law and order," with draconian penalties designed as a deterrent. All these developments may have important political implications for the sustainability of democracy, unless appropriate corrective measures are taken.

The countries of the region are indeed at a crossroads. The successful running of a democracy is neither easy nor automatic. It depends on a number of domestic and external factors. Several decades will have to pass before the fate of this region is known. Will it become a Europeanized, democratic network of friendly states, with frontiers open to free flows of goods, capital, expertise, technology, and labour, and an acceptable standard of living for the vast majority of its people? Or will it become a region of poverty and turmoil, governed by new autocratic regimes assisted to power by diverse forces, separated from the mainstream of the democratic societies not by the Iron Curtain of old, but by a new, "golden curtain" drawn by the West?

Notes

1. An interesting contribution to the debates on the character of the systemic changes in the former socialist countries came from the celebrated sociologist S.N. Eisenstadt. Analysing the character of "velvet revolutions" in the CEE countries in the late 1980s and early 1990s, he declared, "These revolutions were not oriented against 'traditional' pre-modern, or even modernising regimes. They were not rebellious protests against traditional authoritarian regimes, against a divine right of kings, made in the name of modernity and enlightenment. Rather, they constituted a rebellion and protest against what was increasingly perceived by large sectors of the Eastern European societies as a blockage or the distortion of modernity, effected by totalitarian regimes." The Hungarian scholar J. Bognár offered a different interpretation, arguing that "the changes in Central and Eastern Europe can be regarded as a *conservative-liberal revolution*. It constitutes a revolution because ownership, the economic 'subsystem,' power relations and the social structure all undergo deep, rapid, and radical changes. The revolution is conservative because it replaces the statesocialist system with a restored national-cum-religious value system. It strives to establish the predominance of a class of property owners (the bourgeoisie) which already exists or needs to be formed, and it joins conservative schools of thought on current international developments."
2. Jacques Baudot, "Criteria and values for assessing the quality of economic systems."
3. Mihály Simai, "The democratic process and the market: Key aspects of the transition in comparative perspective."
4. György Jenei, "Establishment of an independent, neutral civil service in the former socialist countries of Central and Eastern Europe."
5. Oleg Bogomolov, "Interrelations between political and economic change in Russia and the CIS countries. A comparative analysis."
6. Youri M. Matseiko, "Interactions between political and economic factors in the democratic transformation of Ukraine."
7. Ivan Grdešić, "The politics of privatization in Croatia: Transition in times of war."
8. Ján Morovic, "Political and economic factors in the democratic transformation of Slovakia: Achievements and problems."
9. Kálmán Kulcsár, "The changing political system and realities in Hungary."
10. Janusz Golebiowski, "The political economy of democratization in the Polish transition."
11. Iván Vitányi, "Issues and experiences in the practice of democratization: Models and paradigms."

Systemic and political change, and economic transformation

1

Criteria and values for assessing the quality of economic systems

Jacques Baudot

The truism that an economy is an inherent part of the society in which it operates has consequences that are not always fully understood. An economic system, whether it is a market, planned, or mixed economy, is not an autonomous sphere that can be the subject of a detached and objective science. It is a social construct. It both reflects and influences the norms and values of a society, the aspirations of people, and obviously, the structures and *modus operandi* of power relationships.

This means that a particular economic arrangement – a system, its positive and negative features and its overall quality – have to be assessed with social criteria, within a framework of a political and moral philosophy. Debates, judgements, policies, and actions that affect an economy are always shaped by technical, political, and moral criteria and convictions. The contention here, however, is that a democratic society requires democratic debate on how its economy functions, and that such debate is facilitated by the sharing of clear, explicit criteria and values. Before outlining some of these, it is useful to recall the dominant features of the current economic scene.

Economic conditions vary immensely throughout the world. There are enormous differences among countries and regions in level of income, degree of modernization, use of technology, quality and density of infrastructure, capacity for saving and investment, property rights, and aspects of their legal frameworks, not to mention the availability of institutions such as schools and universities for acquiring skills. Vast numbers of people struggle day by day to make a livelihood by subsistence farming or in the urban "informal" sector. A few acquire money and power by speculative activities, only remotely connected to the production and exchange of goods and services. The existence of a few products of mass consumption that are available all over the world should not be taken as evidence of any significant lessening of the differences in economic and living conditions.

Yet this diverse and unequal world, more like a great Tower of Babel than a global village, has a few strong economic features in common. Most countries have adopted some form of market economic system, with the two basic characteristics of a regime of private ownership and emphasis on freedom of enterprise. This system exists in many specific variants. Most European countries, for instance, really have mixed economies with a strong role for the state and a dense array of regulations. But the central role of the market is almost universally declared. Few government agencies, in developed or developing countries, would think of applying the concept of planning to their efforts to influence the directions of the economic and social processes driven by market forces. When Russia and the countries of Central and Eastern Europe entered their "transition" a few years ago, there was no shadow of doubt, there or in the rest of the world, that the prospect and objective were to create a market economy. To dare even to ask what the transition was "to" was to be hopelessly behind the times and indicative of crypto-communism. The market, as an institution and a symbol of freedom, efficiency, and prosperity, has been enjoying its heyday. By the end of the decade it has been better understood that markets, as other fundamental institutions of society, need to be shaped by norms, which exclude or at least reduce greed, incompetence, and irresponsibility on the part of the private actors and as a minimum, the sharing of a perception of what is right or wrong in the functioning of markets should enable societies to assess the quality of their economic life.

It is again the market, in its incarnation of global capitalism, that forms the overwhelmingly dominant practice and ideology in relationships between nations and regions. A wave of "liberalization," "deregulation," and "privatization" swept across the United States and Europe towards the end of the 1970s, and then engulfed the rest of the world with remarkable speed and force. Structural adjustments, reforms of the economy and flexibility of the labour market have ensued. Critically important in this neo-liberal praxis and ideology is the free circulation of capital. Foreign direct investment has grown from some $5 billion at the beginning of the 1960s to close to $200 billion today. The value of foreign-exchange transactions has jumped from $15 billion a day in the 1970s to a formidable $1,000 billion a day in the late 1990s. Obviously, this free circulation of capital, coupled with a very strong increase in the volume of world trade, is not synonymous with a world without borders. Technologies still do not move freely, and above all, people, or labour to use an economic term, are not allowed to seek economic opportunities in the land of their choice. The huge migrations that marked the world economy towards the beginning of the twentieth century, have no equivalent in the modern version of global capitalism. Yet capitalism as a universal ambition, in symbiosis with the triumph of the market economy as a practice and an ideal, is the driving force behind international relations as this millennium draws to a close.

So the market economy in its various incarnations and global capitalism as a reality and a project are what need to be debated, assessed, and appraised, with clear criteria based on a common political and moral philosophy.

There are four criteria that seem relevant to assessing how an economic system functions: (i) the system should provide work opportunities and sufficient income to the maximum number of people; (ii) the same system should create and liberate enough resources for public institutions to fulfil their collective responsibilities and promote the common good; (iii) workers, employers, citizens, and groups in civil society should be able to participate in the functioning of the economy, whether at corporate, national, or international level; (iv) finally, the economy should leave to individuals enough space and time for pursuits other than earning their livelihood, in the intellectual, artistic, or spiritual domains, or simply for social intercourse and celebration of the pleasures of being human and part of a community.

These quite simple criteria need to be shaped and oriented by a political and moral philosophy. This philosophy emphasizes the use of reason, the practice of moderation in political endeavours, a conviction that individuals and societies are perfectible, and an awareness that errors, lapses, and ill-will can be expected from individuals and from the collective. To put matters more precisely, there are some especially important attitudes and values that may help to make good use of the criteria just mentioned when assessing the prevalent economic system. Here I shall mention only some of them.

It must be realized, of course, that there is no perfect economy, or perfect society. Some are better than others, in time and space. The litmus test of a good society is the prevalence of respect for human dignity. Another important historical conclusion is that progress – improvements in an economic system or in any human institution – will be short-lived if it is forcibly imposed. The rule of law is a necessity for any society, but laws and regulations have to be democratically created. They are effective and respected only when backed by social norms, codes of behaviour, and internalized values expressive of a tradition, a culture, and a willingness to be part of a community, whether a village, a nation, or the world. Politics is a domain of activity, a professional practice in a sphere of society, but it is also a dimension of the functioning of all institutions and of most facets of human relations. To reiterate the initial point, the economy is *par excellence* political, a sphere of society shaped by political power and relationships. Obviously the global economy is no exception in this respect. It is not a luxury, or an extension of a political opinion held by some but not others, to seek equity, to aspire to social justice, primarily in economic terms. It is not only a matter of distribution and redistribution policy, but the essence of a democratic society. All issues of social integration, cohesion, marginalization, and dichotomy, of a divided world, are variations on the theme of the need for social justice. This itself is based on the observation and conclusion that human beings share a common humanity and a common aspiration for at least the most basic sense of dignity. The availability of options for individuals and of room for institutions, including governments, to manoeuvre is a critical aspect of an open and harmonious society. So any form of determinism ought to be rejected *a priori*, for reasons of intellectual discipline and political freedom. "Trends" reflect and express choices. Even those who believe history is providential, directed by a benevolent God, leave room for human freedom and responsibility. Often such room for thought and action appears to be denied by those who see the all-powerful forces, directing the destiny of humanity, in science and technology or in the appetite for comfort and material goods, and the satisfaction of needs, wants, and desires. Often "constraints" are another name for entrenched interests and conservatism. Progress, on the other hand, starts with imagination and generosity of spirit. Equally important is respect for facts and rigour of analysis. It is rare for data and statistics to capture all the dimensions of a phenomenon, which is precisely why efforts should be made to expand their scope. Reflection and democratic debate are enhanced by attending to facts and figures. There is a need for data on poverty and on wealth, for facts on exclusion and on the new élites, for information on the informal sector and on tax evasion and tax avoidance. Averages are often misleading when policies are being designed to produce a good distribution of opportunities and income. It is timely to reaffirm that an efficient, fair tax system is a critical condition for a good economy and a decent society.

These criteria, values, and orientations need to be applied to attempting an overall assessment of the performance of the market economic system. Making such an assessment, globally or in a national setting, is not just an entertaining exercise in political economy. It is and should be done by governments, political parties, trade unions, employers' federations, and the various groups and institutions of a civil society. Naturally (perhaps hopefully), judgements and diagnoses of how an economy is functioning vary according to the tools applied, the weight attached to various features and problems, and the political inclinations of the observers and practitioners. Democracy constitutes an orderly confrontation of various viewpoints and assessments. It does not imply that there is a consensus on the relevance of the various criteria to be applied. However, it does assume there is agreement on a few basic values, including respect for others and an understanding that individual interests need to harmonize with the search for the common good.

A market economy, in theory and in practice, is the best system for enabling people to exert their initiative and creativity. It provides opportunities for work and income and it gives access to material goods and comfort to increasing numbers of people, through technical innovation and rising productivity. Globally, a considerable number of individuals and families are obviously better off materially than they were a few decades ago. Some nations, groups, and individuals have been left out of the benefits of efficient markets and economic growth, but it is possible to take corrective measures. The public authorities have a responsibility to correct the imbalances and inequities created by the functioning of the market. Indeed a good market economy always displays a dense array of institutions and modes of behaviour that facilitate economic transactions and initiatives with full respect for the law and with a strong ethical content. Economies of an anarchic type, with uncivilized or criminal facets, eventually run into trouble. The social fabric cannot resist the pressures created by unregulated markets.

Looking back over past centuries, the capacity of the market economic system to provide people with better living conditions amidst relative freedom is reasonably clear and difficult to challenge. None the less, recent developments in the developed market economies and the former communist and socialist countries are troubling. Everywhere from the United States to Russia and from the United Kingdom to Hungary, poverty and inequality have been increasing, sometimes dramatically. Could the main explanation for this be that the market economy is degenerating into market fundamentalism, so that the balance between labour and capital is upset, causing unbridled capitalism? Many governments have been abdicating their responsibilities and becoming docile instruments of the market, merely a convenient abstraction that masks very specific interests. Elsewhere, the failure of centrally planned economies was construed as evidence that free markets would suffice to ensure economic prosperity. "Reforms" were undertaken as if transferring assets from public to private hands were the alpha and omega of a good market economy. Experts and advisers from prestigious institutions gave an aura of technical soundness and legitimacy to policies that were often no more than crude expressions of greed and spoliation of collective goods and property. Conspicuous wealth, extreme poverty and despair, corruption, criminality, and widespread alienation are the natural concomitants. A market economy needs a good and efficient government to flourish and be able to provide work and income to the maximum number of people. Unregulated markets without strong codes of ethics simply give a free rein to the most questionable human appetites.

As for providing public institutions with sufficient resources to fulfil their responsibilities and promote the common good, this is not a natural virtue inherent in the market economic system. The inherited, traditional functions of government in the Western market economies – overall administration, public order, justice, and defence – make up a declining share of total public expenditure: about 10 per cent in the 1990s. The bulk of this expenditure – between 50 and 70 per cent – is now devoted to social areas, including (in order of importance) education, health, social security, and housing subsidies. Lastly, governments of Western countries spend about 10 per cent of their budgets on supporting their economies, through public investment and subsidies to firms. As elsewhere, this expenditure in these countries absorbs a rising proportion of GNP: about 10 per cent at the beginning of the century, 30 per cent in 1960, and 50 per cent in the 1990s. To finance such levels of public spending, most governments have borrowed, so that public debt has sometimes reached 75 per cent of GNP, as it did in Western Europe in 1995. Such public debt is now limited to 60 per cent of GNP by the Maastricht Treaty. There are several reasons, including the expected level of social security in a developed economy and ageing of the population, why countries in Central and Eastern Europe are heading in the same direction and experiencing comparable problems. Many observers and policy makers interpret this to mean that the welfare state and welfare society are in crisis. The argument goes that taxes have reached a maximum permissible level in most developed societies. The only solution is to ask less from governments and more from markets and private sources of financing. This is also taken to mean that less ought to be spent on adjusting incomes and other forms of inequality. Support for the arts, or the construction of buildings or prestige monuments, should be abandoned, or likewise left to private initiative and largesse. On an international level, there is a dwindling element of public transfer from the rich to the poor expressed through official development assistance, which is being increasingly questioned and criticized. The proposed solution to the problems of the economically underdeveloped countries is private foreign investment. There are no international taxes – except to finance the core administrative budgets of international organizations and the peace-keeping operations of the Security Council and the United Nations General Assembly. A meaningful discussion of how to finance global issues such as protection of the environment, the prevention and cure of epidemics like HIV-AIDS, the prevention of terrorism, or the fight against drug trafficking and other forms of international organized crime, is not even at an initial stage.

Does this mean the market economic system is unable to generate and earmark enough resources for public institutions to make transfers to the needy, finance public goods, and address common problems? Does this mean, for instance, that people will have to pay for their own education and only have access to medical care if they take a private insurance? Does it mean that protection of the environment will eventually depend on the goodwill of prosperous private firms and benevolent governments? Will rich individuals, and then entire cities and regions, hire private police and private armies to protect themselves from the poor, the deprived, and the outlawed? The assumption that public money will become increasingly scarce, at all levels, conjures up all sorts of strange and unattractive scenarios. It is all but certain, for the foreseeable future and within the assumptions made by most democratic regimes, that a utilitarian philosophy will preside over the generation and allocation of public funds. It is unlikely that any great things comparable to the pyramids, the European cathedrals, the Great Wall of China, or even St Petersburg, Angkor Wat, or Versailles will ever be built again. They were the products of regimes with no concern for economic, social, and cultural rights, and no parliamentary debate on taxation. It is highly probable that individuals and families with average and above average incomes will increasingly have to finance themselves, wholly or in part, to obtain services such as education and health. It is hard to imagine levels of taxation at which governments, and in the near future regional and international organizations, could finance both public services and transfers and public goods. Yet it is also highly probable that taxes will have to rise everywhere, even in the least social-democratic and welfare-oriented countries. The current dominant ideology of lower taxes, less social solidarity, and more consumption, is bound to lead to catastrophes. What many societies have achieved in the way of compatible, decent levels of private and public consumption and investment, through a complex, sometimes messy mix of market mechanisms and public regulation, is being destroyed by an ideology that turns global capitalism and individualism into the ultimate rationale of human endeavour.

Participation in the management of an economy and the functioning of a society is an elusive concept. As usual, it is the negative notions and situations – alienation, manipulation, and exploitation – that are easier to grasp and define. The opportunities for initiative, work, and income that the market economy is best at promoting unquestionably form an initial, critical type of participation. Such participation suffers as unemployment and underemployment increase. At workplace level, market economies, particularly in Europe, have contained a wide variety of arrangements and innovations for workers and employees to have a say in decisions affecting their daily lives and the future of their firms. Some of these experiments have found their way into laws and regulations, while others have died. The decline of trade unions, the changes in production structures that technological innovation and the mobility of capital enable, and the ubiquitous rise of the service sector in modern economies are factors that militate

34

against participation. So does the emphasis on flexibility, the need for employers to hire and dismiss people as the exigencies of competition and the demands of the market dictate.

At another level of analysis, is there a tendency today towards a concentration of economic, financial, and political power? There are conflicting signs. Symbolic institutions such as "G7 plus one," or the strength and global reach of transnational corporations, indicate indeed that there is a strong concentration of power. This is not offset by international trade unions or non-governmental organizations, or checked by international organizations with a democratic base and a universalist mandate. Democracy at the international level is in its infancy. There is no transparency in the operations of transnational corporations and financiers, let alone accountability to the people of the world. National parliaments also have very limited participation in the decisions affecting national economies and their integration into the regional or global market. People are increasingly active in associations and organizations that represent a cause or a set of specific interests. People are also more involved in international affairs. Indeed people in a growing number of countries are able to delegate their parcel of sovereignty to their representatives in the legislative and executive branches. But with a few exceptions, regular political parties are not thriving, and in some places ground is being gained by extremist movements with totalitarian ideologies. Many public institutions have problems of legitimacy and credibility. Political "consumers" outnumber informed and responsible citizens. Many education systems are in trouble. It is unclear when and how the market economies, in a context of globalization, will encourage people to devote time and energy to the various forums in which the future of the world is shaped.

Working to make a livelihood and participating in managing the economy and society are demanding tasks. Most people in the world simply struggle to survive. The public authorities are either remote or threatening to most of them. So is it a sign of ignorance, idealism, or élitism to claim that a good economic system should provide individuals and communities with time and space to indulge in leisure and the pursuit of intellectual, artistic, and spiritual ventures? Taking as an example the countries of Central and Eastern Europe, can there be any other legitimate, urgent goal except an efficient and competitive market economy, when GNP has dropped by 20 per cent in four years and 1989 production is unlikely to be matched again before 2000? In any case, is it not obvious that the market economic system is the one that scores best by this last criterion? Has not this system, through its long, painful, often ghastly history, managed to liberate most men, women, and children from slavery, forced labour, and the worst forms of exploitation? Does it not reflect well on the market economy and political democracy that women are on their way to personal autonomy and equality, that working hours have been reduced, that many domestic and other tasks have been made easier and quicker, that illiteracy is receding, and that increasing numbers of people have access to knowledge and information through television, the Internet, and even tourism? There is no other economic system, runs this line of argument, that can provide people with such a good combination of material comfort, freedom, and time for leisure and other pursuits.

All this is probably true. At this juncture in history, given the discredit that totalitarian excesses have inflicted on more generous doctrines and Utopias, the liberation of humanity from deprivation and the constraints of ignorance will best be promoted by building efficient market economies. It is even conceivable, in the not too distant future, that the logic of the market may become less adverse to the logic of giving. For this path to open for more than a privileged few, it is necessary to slow down and diversify the process of globalization and economic integration immediately, to fight the ideology of global capitalism, to be merciless with various forms of concentration of economic and financial power, including the media, to promote and defend a rich array of institutions, to affirm a continuum between private morality and public virtue, to free scientific research and other human endeavours from the grip of a monetization that destroys the social fabric, and perhaps above all, to proclaim *urbi et orbi* that all human beings share a common humanity, so that respect for others and social justice are moral and political imperatives.

Reference

Colette, Jean-Michel (1997), *L'évolution des dépenses publiques et le poids de l'Etat dans les principaux pays d'Europe occidental*, Rapports et Documents, Genève-Gex: Foyer Européen de la Culture.

2

The democratic process and the market: Key aspects of the transition in comparative perspective

Mihály Simai

Ideologies and realities

In the bipolar world of the Cold War, most Western politicians and political scientists drew a simplified distinction, dividing the world into market-economic democracies and etatist, totalitarian regimes. The Western industrial countries saw themselves as true democracies, while the countries of Eastern Europe, and most developing countries, were classed as totalitarian, autocratic, or dictatorial. Many of their counterparts in the East applied a similar simplification when they viewed the division of the world.

The issues of democracy and human rights occupied an important place in the global political and ideological struggles of the period. Civil and political rights took priority in Western countries, while the etatist, socialist regimes of the East laid emphasis, in their debates with the West, on economic and cultural rights. However, in practical terms the Western world contained no static, democratic market systems with universal characteristics. The region containing what are known today as the European transition economies, the new democracies, or the new market economies has never been politically or economically homogeneous.[1] Mainly due to pressure from the Soviet Union, they were strongly inclined to introduce universalist institutional patterns in their political and economic systems.[2] However, important distinctions between them persisted, due to differences in level of development, cultural tradition, and previous history. This diversity became steadily stronger after the death of Stalin and the Hungarian Revolution of 1956. While some Central and Eastern European (CEE) states became more liberal and less oppressive, others maintained or even tightened their dictatorial regimes.

A similar simplification was made in evaluating the economic systems. The debates on national, institutional, and global changes were influenced by two Utopian extremes. One is the Soviet model: economic development is to be managed by the state and subservient to a collective will ostensibly represented by the hand of central government. (Interestingly, Marx never denied in his writings the historical role of the market in the development process. According to his analysis, the market was the solvent that would break down the traditional rigidities of society and allow development.) The other extreme is a liberal Utopia, where the "invisible hand" of the market is master. The role of the state is confined to safeguarding property rights and removing obstacles to the efficient operation of markets. Advocates of this ideology attribute allocative inefficiencies to market failures, caused by strong state intervention. Both these extreme views have a high ideological content, and have proved themselves counter-productive.

Capitalism has never been a closed, homogeneous political, economic, and ideological system. It has provided the socio-economic foundations for a variety of economic models, political structures, and ideologies. Some of these have been decidedly unresponsive to fundamental social problems which others have recognized at an early stage. The capitalist system has also been able to accommodate some fanatical ideologies, such as violent nationalism and fascism, which are sadly gaining ground again in some parts of the world. Their divisive doctrines of racism, ethnic hatred, and religious bigotry are fuelled by mounting socio-economic problems and political stalemate, but cannot in any way promote global solutions to problems of poverty, environmental degradation, or crime.

Markets played an interesting role in the history of the socialist countries. In Soviet Russia, Lenin himself initiated a market-driven regime, the New Economic Policy, after the short period of "war communism." This in turn was superseded towards the end of the 1920s, but it continued to inspire many socialist reformers and advocates of market socialism. Even Stalin accepted that instruments of the "socialist market" were needed in economic policy. Some elements and forms of market exchange persisted in almost all socialist countries, but they were specific, being confined to certain niches and instruments within the system. Even where they were widespread, they were strongly distorted. The main source of information was the central plan, which the actors in the economy received as mandatory targets, through a system in which central targets and "plan-bargaining" were the dominating factor. Price signals played a very limited role in the state sector. Even in the socialist countries where major reforms were introduced, prices were subordinated to social or economic goals and priorities determined by the political process. These goals were not constant. The socialist system relied on constant redistribution of income through the budget, so that efficiently functioning parts of the economy surrendered most of their gains to subsidize the rest of the economy, including consumers. The market was dominated by strong state monopolies. The other, restricted component of the market was the private sector. Its size and legal status varied from country to country – even by orders of magnitude by 1989, on the eve of the systemic changes. The private sector relied on filling supply gaps left by the state sector and on the goodwill of the authorities. In some countries, much private market exchange was illegal and the actors subject to prosecution. In others it was tolerated within a range of legal limits.

There was also an important international dimension to market forces in the socialist countries. They remained part of the global economy, even though their domestic institutions and the patterns of their international economic relations tended to isolate them from global markets.[3] The institutions of the centrally planned economic system developed a bias against external economic relations. The economic policies of the socialist countries reinforced the inward-looking character of the development process, over a period of several decades. Indeed new economic foundations of nationalism were established or reinforced in all the countries of the Soviet bloc. This became probably the largest economic grouping in history to drop out of the global market system for geostrategic and systemic reasons. However, although the system was institutionally isolated from the world market, the judgement of the world market had indirect influences on the socialist countries, through the high prices they paid for new technology, their losses through the terms of trade, and the high cost of debt servicing. The world market also had some influence on the prices in trade among the socialist countries.

The economic interactions of the socialist bloc with the rest of the world reached its lowest point in the 1950s. Thereafter, the emergence of the third world and of the détente process introduced forces and mechanisms that intensified economic relations with countries outside the bloc. Even so, they remained largely isolated, for about 40 years, from the integrating forces of global capital and technology flows and from the prospect of more favourable trading conditions. This isolation also arose out of the strategic considerations applied by the West. Meanwhile there was some intensification of economic relations between the CEE countries and the Soviet Union, although the institutional level of cooperation remained rather primitive and inefficient. Efforts to harmonize economic development among them through a planned international division of labour largely failed, although some elements of specialization arose.[4] Some market instruments were introduced with the reforms in certain socialist countries, but a shift towards closer integration or reintegration into global markets became possible only with the change of system in the early 1990s.[5]

The existing differences between the socialist countries were also responsible, to some extent, for the various ways in which their etatist-socialist regimes collapsed,[6] and for the spectrum of CEE post-communist regimes that emerged. These differed in the way their markets developed, and in the character of the political regimes, including the progress made with establishing a civil society and the depth and stability of democracy.

A new chapter of regional history opened with the collapse of the etatist-socialist CEE regimes and dismemberment of the Soviet Union. The relatively swift transition to a competitive market system and pluralist political democracy in the region constitutes a historically unprecedented task. Its outcome depends largely on harmonizing its economic and political aspects, which have often proved conflicting in the past.

Relations between the influence of market forces and the development of democracy have never been simple or straightforward. Many politicians, scholars, and others have therefore taken the postulates of a sustainable democratic political system and a theoretically efficient "undistorted" market to be conflicting, contradictory categories. The American scholar Lester C. Thurow, in his best-selling book *The Future of Capitalism*, writes, "Democracy and capitalism have very different beliefs about the proper distribution of power. One believes in a completely equal distribution of power, 'one man one vote,' while the other believes that it is the duty of the economically fit to drive the unfit out of business and into economic extinction."[7] He adds that over the past couple of centuries, two factors have allowed these two power systems to coexist as democratic capitalism. First, it has always been possible to convert economic power to political power, or political power to economic power. Secondly, government has been actively used to alter market outcomes and generate a fairer distribution of income than the market alone would produce. Thurow also raises doubts about the sustainability of this balancing act, in an era when market forces are producing much greater inequalities. The debates about the sustainability of the democratic process in a competitive market system, as indicated by Thurow, are very old of course. Democracy, as it is basically understood, is not a political ideology like liberalism, communism, socialism, or Nazism. It is not a set of political ideas about the values, instruments, goals, and outcomes of social actions. It describes a particular system of government and the distribution of power within such a system. In fact most political ideologies use the concept of democracy, with qualifications based on their specific views and preferences. Liberal democracies place constitutional limits on government power, safeguard civil liberties, and are representative in the sense that office and power are gained by competitive elections. The original meaning of social democracy was the principle of equality in society, including equality of wealth.

The progress of democracy was a lengthy process in most of the developed industrial countries. It was influenced by social and economic interests and conflicts, by political ideologies, by ethnic problems, and by external and internal factors and forces in each country. Democratic rights expanded progressively, often after bitter social and political conflict. Practically speaking, the spread of democracy in most cases followed on from the growing prosperity of the people, containment of social conflict through reform, and growing social mobility. The contradiction between a declared or constitutionally guaranteed equality of rich and poor and substantial inequalities in the distribution and redistribution of the national cake remained unmanageable while the cake was small. So an important question often asked about poorer countries is what type of democracy they can develop and sustain. The capitalist system in very poor countries has not been able to sustain democracy without major setbacks. Capitalism and democracy in the second half of the twentieth century have coexisted well where there were no major social tensions or conflicts and the systems could introduce significant social reforms. Events in several European countries, as in Germany in the first half of the twentieth century have shown that a democratic system can be undermined by intolerance, ideological fundamentalism, violent nationalism, or internal or external events, forces and factors that create intolerable economic problems and unsustainable inequalities in society.

Historically, the markets in different countries have also resulted from a long process of organic development. There has been an interaction between the specific features of these societies and of their markets. The societies have also created the legal framework and the various organizations required for the market to function properly. On the other hand, external factors have also played an important part in market development and growth. Markets have played a multiple role in the history of their countries. They have promoted an increase in the number of social groups and interests like the emergence of the modern enterpreneurial middle class, the managerial élite, the modern working class with its different strata, the professional élite, or the modern state bureaucracy. This process also served to underpin political diversity and pluralism. They have also promoted a concentration of economic power, monopolies, and oligopolies and thereby a concentration of influence on the political power structure. Then they have promoted a separation of the economy from politics, and played a corrective role in cases of government failure. At the same time they have failed in many areas, necessitating corrective government intervention. All this points to the need to understand the historical environment in which the market and the political process interact.

Historical evidence shows that the development of a market economy normally preceded democratic changes in governance. There are very few cases where pluralist, liberal, democratic systems emerged before there was a market economy with clearly defined, transparent property rights, dispersed economic power, free entry and exit, and a non-discriminatory system of economic competition.

On the other hand, democracy has not necessarily been a prerequisite for an effective market system, or for economic development. Empirical evidence suggests that authoritarian governments are often less vulnerable to special-interest groups or ethnic or regional pressures when implementing major socio-economic policies or carrying out painful structural reforms. Sustaining the democratic methods of governance has proved particularly difficult and often disadvantageous in troubled times. Non-democratic regimes are often able to create higher savings, through enforced public savings and other measures. The concept of a "development dictatorship" has often been cited as an excuse for the dictatorial regimes in some South-East Asian countries. The pre-war patterns in Central and Eastern Europe also demonstrated that market economies could coexist with a range of political systems, dictatorial or democratic. (Thurow mentions in his book that American capitalism managed to coexist with slavery.) Of course a thorough cost-benefit analysis of non-democratic regimes would question the allocative efficiency of some totalitarian regimes, and the preferences given to various groups in the ruling élite or the army. The political and social costs of non-democratic regimes have been very high in many cases, compared with their favourable influence on some economic indicators.

Through the long history of human efforts to achieve it, democracy has been interpreted in practice in various ways. It has been seen as an ideal political system, unattainable in full, a set of political institutions for sustaining or changing the political establishment by regular elections, a system that only functions when based on a broad middle class and a developed civil society, and so on. Democracy as an ideal and an actual system has changed over the more than 2,000 years since its "invention." In the twentieth century, there are several important conditions that need to be fulfilled for the democratic process to succeed. Success in this case simply means that the democratic process will be capable of reproducing itself, without creating situations that require or elicit non-democratic methods of governance.

Some of these conditions have related to the characteristics of the political élite. These aspects have been dealt with by such diverse personalities as Socrates, Thomas Paine, or James Madison. In the twentieth century, when personal selection and often the victory of a candidate in the political process depends in many countries on campaign funding, it has become even more important that those elected to parliament or local or national office should be of relatively high quality and reasonably honest. Democratic systems do not produce automatically more experienced and responsive politicians than other systems.

Another set of conditions for the success of a democratic system concerns the prevalent political attitudes, the political culture. This aspect of democracy is particularly important in Central and Eastern Europe where it was shaped by decades of dictatorial regimes influenced by militant ideologies. There must be democratic self-control

43

and tolerance by the majority, and by the minority. Effective contests for leadership in successful democratic systems require a certain level of tolerance of otherness. There are two particularly important conditions related to the institutional patterns. One relates to the scope of governance by democratically elected institutions. This should be relatively limited, so that it can be handled by the mechanisms of democracy, whereas the totalitarian decision-making of many non-democratic governing structures makes the use of non-democratic instruments essential. The other is the need for a well-trained, respected, professional, and competent bureaucracy. This must be fairly constant, to offset the non-specialist politicians.

One of the most delicate sets of conditions for the success and sustainability of democracy relates to socio-economic problems. Some political scientists have suggested that if a society is not in reasonable health, democracy can be not only risky but disastrous.[8] History has also shown that there has to be a certain degree of justice and participation and a fair distribution of welfare to sustain democracy. Democracy cannot be sustained where the distribution of the national cake is a zero-sum game and there is large-scale exclusion. Democracy cannot be treated in isolation from other social or economic processes. At the end of the twentieth century, democratization must also be viewed from global perspectives, for it is increasingly taken as a universal international or global process, closely related to global socio-political changes, especially the international and universal character of human rights. It must include the world's macro and micro-processes: the character of inter-state relations, and the commitments of the main powers to building and sustaining a democratic world. It is also increasingly evident that the micro global processes cannot be controlled and managed from global centres or by regional and national bureaucracies. The importance of grassroots institutions, organizations, and activities is increasing. Some ideologists of globalization, such as John Naisbitt,[9] suggest that globalization increases the scope for small groups or firms, because they have greater flexibility than larger units. According to Naisbitt, the essence of the global paradox is that the more global or universal humanity becomes, the more "tribally" people act. This reduces the traditional role of the state and changes its functions. "Now, with the electronics revolution, both representative democracy and economies of scale are obsolete. Now everyone can have efficient direct democracy."[10] The fragmentation process, however, is not just a result of the "new tribalism." It also derives from the marginalization and exclusion that emanate from the highly unequal character of the globalization process.

Interrelations between market-building and democratization, during and after the transition

There is always a danger of simplification when analysing interrelations between political and economic processes. A relatively short time has elapsed since the systemic changes in Central and Eastern Europe, and the speed of progress in the economic, political, and institution-building processes has differed. This makes it almost impossible to provide a detailed, credible, documented comparative analysis of the interrelations between the economic changes and the development of democracy in the former socialist countries. However, a few general observations can be made: (i) there have often been different forces behind the processes in different countries, which in itself has resulted in more divergence than convergence; (ii) in most cases, the two processes have taken place in parallel, and the interactions have mainly been indirect; (iii) the development of democracy has been influenced by the character of the regimes that preceded the change of system; (iv) the influence of external, international factors and forces has been important to the economic and the political transformation, but the interactions of the two processes have seldom been surveyed in a systematic way. The international organizations assigned by the main industrial powers to "command" the transition process have developed several important "transition indicators." These include political democratization, establishment of a new legal framework for the economy, particularly in competition and liberalizing market entry, macroeconomic stabilization, monetary and fiscal reforms, price liberalization, liberalization of trade and foreign exchange, banking reform and interest-rate liberalization, restructuring of enterprises, introducing effective corporate governance, market-building, with special emphasis on labour and capital markets, and integration into global markets based on openness. All have placed strong emphasis on privatization, dismantling the economic system of central planning, and creating a new business élite. Liberalization and the introduction of free-market policies have been among the most important aids to reintegrating the former socialist countries into global markets and building up new contractual relationships with the Bretton Woods institutions. The democratic agenda was almost ignored in the early years of the transition process, when shock therapy and the remedies of the multilateral financial institutions were being put forward.[11]

The character of the evolving political systems

Totalitarian, one-party regimes involve above all important limitations on individual freedom. So the collapse of the totalitarian state resulted in almost unrestricted freedom, as one of the first steps in the democratization process, in a number of CEE countries. This was an inevitable reaction to the past. Individual freedom was taken to be the fundamental requirement for progress in building a civil society, the emergence and development of various social and political groups, and provision of chances for these to articulate their interests and values. In almost all the European post-socialist countries, apart from some that emerged through the disintegration of a poly-ethnic state, freedom now prevails in the literal sense. Censorship has vanished and anyone with the means may publish a newspaper, leaflet, or book. There is practically unlimited freedom of association, and numerous political parties and trade unions are active. This process has taken place much faster than it did in the Western countries, but there have been practically no moral, ethical, and institutional constraints upon it. So the result in many cases has been anarchic conditions. Among the important economic drawbacks have been the rapid development and spread of the black economy, the disappearance of tax-paying discipline, and neglect for the interests of consumers. The loosening of government controls has opened the door to criminal elements on a scale unprecedented in the history of capitalism. The variety of capitalism that is developing in Russia, for example, is one of the most greedy and lawless systems ever seen in any country. However, such "gangster economics" or "klepto-capitalism" is not confined to Russia.

The rule of law has been considered another fundamental postulate of the political transformation in societies where the ruling party was "above the law" and arbitrary decisions and government decrees provided the bulk of the institutional framework. The law in a democratic society is an important instrument for social control of the whole population within a jurisdiction. In the totalitarian one-party state, the ruling party was above the law, which gave almost unlimited power to it and to its executive arms in the power structure. Democratic states have to rest on the rule of law, rather than the rule of police or dictators, to protect personal security and rights, safe-guard personal freedom from arbitrary intervention, and regulate the ways the democratic system functions. New constitutional guarantees were needed to establish the rule of law. One of the main new elements in the constitutions enacted, or in the case of Poland and Hungary, fundamentally amended, is recognition and honour for private ownership as the fundamental form of property-holding. This recognition, which extends to the ownership rights of foreigners as well, is a basic condition for the development of a capitalist market system. An important and controversial issue is the debate on the limitation of ownership related to foreign ownership, especially of land. The law that developed out of the new constitutions has frequently been ill-designed and ill-formulated. There were thousands of rules that had to be replaced or amended. Even in the countries that made the fastest progress with modernizing the law – Poland, Hungary, and the Czech Republic – there have been some major legislative shortcomings. Progress with the legal system has also been complicated by the desire of these three countries to join the European Union.

The new or amended constitutions in the former socialist countries contain provisions for respecting human rights, but there are two major problems in this respect. One relates to economic, social, and cultural rights, which were considered as fundamentally important under the communist regimes. These rights, and particularly the conditions for respecting them in practice, are not so strongly established, and the emphasis has been placed more on political and civil rights. In practical policy terms, the conflicts between the two sets of rights are much greater, of course. People do not want to accept civil and political rights as a trade-off for full employment, social security, free health care, and education. They want both, which has proved to be more or less impossible.

Another source of political and governmental weakness in several former socialist countries has been an ill-defined distribution of power between the head of state, the legislature, and central and local government. This is sometimes due to hasty adoption of constitutions that reflect expedient compromises. In other cases it results from personal power struggles between individuals in high office, or between groups advocating liberalism or autocratic, populist ideologies. The advocates of presidential government dream of complete freedom to select government ministers, the right to issue decrees with the force of law (in other words, bypass the legislature), and relatively wide powers to dissolve awkward parliaments. These are essentially autocratic tendencies that represent serious dangers in many CEE countries, where there are strong regional traditions of autocracy.[12]

Another important factor shaping the character of the political system is the proper distribution of power in the former socialist countries. Here the democratization process and the building of a modern capitalist society are closely related. As Thurow, for instance, describes, power in a modern democratic, capitalist society has two main sources – political and economic, or in more practical terms, political position and wealth. The still brief history of the new system in the former socialist countries has shown how the possibility of converting economic power into political power and vice versa, along with other means of gaining special advantage, is a major source of corruption. This applies especially where the choice of politicians and exercise of social control over them is not based on an "organic," long-term process of selection, where the balance between the executive and the legislature is not well defined, and where the rule of law is not well established. With a massive redistribution of wealth underway, political power was used in almost all these countries on an unprecedented scale to create wielders of economic power. The newly rich, on the other hand, prefer political forces that do not pose a threat to their new wealth. This factor, of course, does not question or deny the democratic credentials of new governments that have been properly elected or the democratic character of the new institutions that sustain a plural society. The holders of political power change as a result of shifting popular votes, and legitimation may be withdrawn from the ones that created the new economic élite. This process will separate the two groups, so that the autonomy of the economic system and the political process increases. There will inevitably be important differences of interest among the various groups in the new entrepreneurial class. They may form differing or contrasting political ideas, goals, and policies, related also to their economic position on the market.

Political competition for power is not confined to a single factor. It has a number of other sources in modern, democratic, capitalist societies. The political process, under the pressure of various social groups – workers, farmers, urban professionals – has created forces that seek to limit or reduce inequalities, and to constrain the role of economic power in the society. Another important factor in the political process is nationalism and xenophobia. A contribution to the political process will also be made by the various value systems, which add qualifications to the concept and practice of democracy, such as Christian, liberal, socialist, social, and perhaps others.

All these problems raise the question of the character of the political parties, their social constituencies, and their relations to the market system. Maintaining political pluralism requires broad consent to the shifts in power resulting from free elections: on the willingness of the ruling party to step down after political defeat, and on the tolerance of the organized opposition for those in power. However, it is equally important that those in power have time and opportunity for genuine dialogue with the electorate, about the latter's concerns and fears, and that they be able to adjust their policies and manage the conflicts that emerge. There is also a necessary minimum readiness for the governing parties and the opposition to cooperate on certain national issues.

Large numbers of political parties sprang up in all the CEE countries after the fall of single-party dictatorship. They can be divided into four groups, according to their origin, two of them consisting of survivals or successor parties. One group of survivals or re-established parties originated from before the communist period. They include the Christian democrats, and various agrarian and social democratic parties. Some represent narrow and even anachronistic interests, and their ideas derive mainly from experiences before the Second World War. The other "survivor" group consists of successors to the former communist party, which in some countries may have split into two groups. The reformers in the old communist party come to resemble modern social democratic parties in Western Europe, while the more conventional, traditional groups remain Marxist. The third group of parties derives from groups that actively opposed the communists: Solidarity in Poland, the Free Democrats (SZDSZ) in Hungary, and a number of others in other countries. The fourth group is mixed. It includes some small, peculiar, and even unique political groups, like the Liberal Democrats in Russia, and the various loyalist groups that seek to restore the monarchy. Some of these parties are "nonpolitical" in character, such as the Greens, the Beer-lovers Party in Poland, or the Independent Erotic Initiative in the Czech Republic. Except for the traditional Marxists and the right-wing populists, most political parties accept and advocate a modern market system, if with some political or ideological qualifications. The etatist traditions in the region have left a strong mark on these ideologies, especially where a party champions a specific group, such as farmers, who were heavily subsidized during the communist regime.

Most political parties have a limited membership. They have more of the nature of electoral parties, which confine themselves between elections to parliamentary activity. In most cases they have no well-defined or articulated interests behind them. Some are parochial parties lacking a vision of modern society. This means that several of them refrain from participating in any national consensus-building. There is little or no mutual confidence among the parties about their attitude to democratic institutions. The level of tolerance of opponents is rather low. Many of the parties collect only a tiny fraction of the vote. Therefore former socialist countries still need modern, integrating parties guided by a vision of a modern society, and advocating lasting moral values. The absence of large social groups with identifiable homogeneous interests and values makes it hard for such parties to emerge. The problems are reflected clearly in the electoral "alliances" put together in some countries, often on an ethnic or religious, rather than a political basis.

The effect of interactions between politics and economic problems on the evolving system

Since political and economic changes had to be implemented by the state, from above, and external political forces and factors also contributed strongly to shaping the transition process, a forceful inter-relationship developed between the two processes. Some of these interrelations favoured both processes, by speeding up the dismantling of the earlier system's institutions and the building of market institutions, including the legal framework for them. The political process gave impetus to private enterprise, by providing the legal and economic conditions it required.

There have been some important achievements in market-building, particularly the two main ones, for labour and capital. The former has developed fairly fast in the CEE countries, where the adjustment process has been facilitated by a relatively educated labour force. The combination of a high educational level and quite low wages made it easier for labour to adapt to the new market conditions and meet a demand. The components of this demand, the occupational patterns, have changed along with the changes in ownership structure, due to privatization, foreign direct investment (FDI), the dismantling of large state enterprises, the low level of new domestic investment, and the patterns of new private enterprise.

All the former socialist countries have encountered more difficulty with building their capital markets, which were absent from the centrally planned economies. The legal framework for building them was influenced by the prevailing economic environment, and by the outside advice received and the pressures for greater liberalization and openness. The role of capital markets – promoting capital accumulation and allocating resources – linked them particularly strongly with the political process, through the state's role in redistribution of income and wealth and creation of a new entrepreneurial élite.

This new business class is rather mixed in content. A relatively small proportion (0.1–3 per cent) can be classed as very rich, even by international standards. There were several patterns behind the creation or expansion of the new entrepreneurial élite in these countries: the development of the legal framework; the introduction of liberal economic policies; assistance with special loans; and above all, redistribution of wealth through the privatization process. The results of integral development of capitalists from the grass roots have tended to be small and medium-sized firms, the owners of which make up about 90 per cent of the entrepreneurial class. About half of these went into business after losing their jobs, as the only way of making a living. In most of the former Soviet republics, the process of creating a new business élite has been highly controversial, and in some areas linked with criminal activity. The Russian mafia may be the world's largest grouping of organized criminals, consisting of about 5,000 gangs with close to 3 million members. They managed to 'privatize' more than two-thirds of the country's retail outlets, hotels, and service operations, notably the banking system.[13]

The development of the foreign-owned sector in the transition economies has also been influenced by political factors. Foreign investors and firms were attracted by the disappearance of the main important political risk factor, the danger of expropriation, and by the low prices of the assets offered during the privatization process. Of course the building of new market institutions, the development of the legal system and establishment of the business infrastructure have been indispensable to the efficient functioning of private firms. The desire to attract foreign investors encouraged faster building of market institutions. Indeed the effort to attract FDI has often given more of an impetus to institutional change than domestic political and economic pressures. To attract FDI, governments had to introduce new legislation on national and foreign entrepreneurship,[14] and various attractive economic policy measures, such as tax concessions or even subsidies. It was also necessary to conclude bilateral agreements with a number of countries on protecting foreign investments and on double taxation. Almost 60 specific, bilateral investment treaties have been concluded so far between the former socialist countries of Europe and the industrial market economies.[15] The increasing importance of foreign capital in some economies resulted in a measure of resentment against foreign ownership, fomented particularly by populist groups on the right and extreme left. Their calls for a "struggle against foreign exploitation" have not had a strong influence on the majority of the population, but may still become a major source of political conflict in the future.

The interactions between the political and economic changes were also responsible for some of the initial problems and difficulties in the transition countries. First, domestic and external political forces were at least partly responsible for the failure to enshrine the postulates of the transition in a logical, rational, generally agreed framework or action programme. This might have laid down optimum sequences of events and facilitated selection of a preferred model for the market economy, on which to base the transition process. There were a number of reasons for this failure, including lack of expertise, limited information on the real patterns in developed industrial countries, ideological preconceptions, and wishful thinking.

The essential role of the state in the transition process led to other important problems in practical terms. Some of the main slogans in the political struggle against communism had been the need to dismantle costly and inefficient bureaucracies, and create democracy, accountability, transparency, freedom from corruption, and so on. The dismantling of the bureaucratic state was expected to reduce radically the transaction costs of society. However, market-building could not be carried out without active government involvement. Indeed the tasks of the transition sometimes increased the powers of the bureaucracy still further, especially in the redistribution of wealth and income, and often with little or no transparency at all. There was very little democratic control over the privatization process in most of the former socialist countries. In several, corruption and other illegal sources of wealth have become major forms of cooperation between the new political and economic élites, and they exerted a big influence on the way the markets started to function.

The greatest and the most conspicuous changes have occurred in the consumer markets. The region constitutes a large consumer market, even though most of the population have low purchasing power. Consumerism is spreading everywhere, with a relatively important group of big-spending successful entrepreneurs, better-paid managers and professionals, and often criminals in the vanguard.

The experiences of the transition economies show that the role of governments, and their functions in the economy as participants, actors, regulators, or agents of change, cannot be examined in isolation from the level of development and its institutional and structural implications. As participants in the world economy, the former socialist countries have far less power than the key industrial countries to deal with the internal consequences of exchange-rate fluctuations and speculative capital movements. They are the "price-takers" in the global economy. Furthermore, they do not have available to them the same accumulated experience and range of policy instruments as the industrial nations.

The costs, benefits, and realities

The progress that most former socialist countries have made towards a democratic market system in less than a decade cannot be overlooked. They have achieved more in this respect than many Western countries did over several decades of earlier development. They have created numerous political and economic institutions and conducted a redistribution of income and wealth that corresponds with a market system.[16] However, there are important differences between them in their success and in the internal cost-benefit structure of the changes, and widening gaps between winners and losers. These countries failed to establish conditions that would promote a more equitable distribution of the inevitable human costs of the transition process. Although the transition is not complete, it has already resulted in heavy economic losses, social disintegration, unemployment, and poverty in almost all the countries. The extent of these losses varies from country to country. About half the CEE population and 75 per cent of people in Russia cannot afford anything beyond their household costs and essential food items. Due to social diseases attributable to the transition process, there has been a decline in human solidarity and courtesy, and a deterioration in human relationships, including family ties, while indifference, egotism, cynicism, dishonesty, vandalism, delinquency, drug abuse, pornography, corruption, crime, and violence are increasing. These are fuelling a popular desire for "law and order" with draconian penalties designed as a deterrent. All these developments may have important political consequences unless appropriate corrective policies are introduced.

Economic stagnation and decline and social deprivation have never provided solid foundations for experiments with democratization and marketization. If the market system and democracy bring inflation, unemployment, mounting inequality, and declining standards of living, the result will be fear, alienation, and distrust. For 40 years, the etatist regimes with their communist promises sought to convince people they needed to sacrifice present welfare for some future gain. Many people have seen a parallel with this in the vague promises made by the new regimes that advocate market reforms and democracy. They are inclined to see the evolving regimes as "redistributive coalitions" for the benefit of a small new minority. The transition process has shown that although the majority support democracy, they do not see marketization or privatization as sufficient or attractive enough goals, especially if they have experienced more of the adverse consequences, while the gains have gone to a narrow stratum in society. In countries where the "post-socialist" coalitions were later voted out of power, the electorate was voting against the increasing poverty and unemployment, the declining standard of living, and the other economic and social difficulties. In some cases this was also a protest vote against the policies of governments and political forces that sought to restore the political and ideological values of pre-war regimes. The socialist parties and their coalition partners were not offering a return to full employment, central planning, or a one-party system. People were not voting for a return to the communist past, but for more equal chances and greater security.

The future of democracy in the region does not depend on economic factors alone. Naturally, the gap between promises and expectations and realities is an important source of political problems. Practically all the former socialist countries have their advocates of autocratic government, and in some countries these forces have been able to manipulate elections, aided by the political apathy of large groups in society. The nostalgia for "law and order" regimes, particularly in countries like Russia, which have large criminal groups, may be a source of support for "neo-authoritarianist" feelings among the people. The ethnic hatreds and conflicts traditionally problematic in the region, coupled with xenophobia and violent nationalism, also pose grave dangers to the democratization process. Moreover, the ethnic problems are often closely related to the redistribution of wealth and income, in all the transition countries. Many minorities are marginalized and locked into a vicious circle of poverty. So the pressures for anti-democratic extremist policies may come from a wide variety of sources.

There are, of course, a number of structural changes that support and sustain democracy in the former socialist countries. The social composition of today's CEE countries is very different from what it was before the Second World War or in the early Cold War period. These are no longer traditional peasant societies, where authoritarian rule can easily be enforced. They have large professional strata, a broad industrial working class, and a small but growing entrepreneurial élite and middle class. There may be political forces that would prefer to limit democracy or have an autocratic regime, but open or disguised political efforts to introduce dictatorship would encounter strong internal opposition. The elections in Slovakia in 1998 or in Romania indicated the resentment against authoritarian regimes or tendencies. A retreat from democracy would also provoke adverse international reactions, which would do great damage to countries that are heavily dependent on their external economic relations.

The role of external factors – Conclusions

External forces and factors have always played an important role in the region, in introducing and sustaining dictatorial regimes and now in the democratization process. In the twentieth century, both the Nazi-oriented and communist regimes in the region had strong external supporters, and were imposed on and sustained by the influence of a dominant foreign power.

Today there are external influences on the political changes coming from a number of sources. (i) There is a strong "demonstration effect" from the Western democratic market systems. This plays a definite, though limited role in creating sustainable democratic systems. (ii) There is the role of various Western institutions, public and private, including foundations and other NGOs that want to help in building democratic institutions. These also have only limited influence, of course, particularly because several transition countries lack a well-structured civil society. There may be more wishful thinking than global reality behind the question "Does democracy travel?" which some scholars have raised recently.[17] (iii) Another factor relates to the issue of external guarantees. The sustainability of democracy depends much on external supports and guarantees, if a society lacks strong democratic forces and an organically developed civil society containing strong advocates of democracy, and has young, inexperienced democratic institutions to handle the inevitable social tensions and conflicts. Here it is most important that there should continue to be no external dictatorial regimes in Europe that could support domestic extremists in the CEE countries. The world of the 1990s is not the world of the 1920s or 1930s. There are no dictatorial regimes among the great Western powers. Apart from the globally important, if unenforceable norms of the UN Charter, there are important guarantees for democracy in institutions such as NATO and the European Union, to which most of the CEE countries aspire to belong.

The postulates for implanting democracy from above and supporting it from outside must not be simplified or confined to formal institutions. It is relatively easy to change the institutional framework of governance by centrally initiated reforms. On the other hand, it is extremely difficult, or well-nigh impossible, to implant a new behavioural infrastructure from above. Introducing a multi-party system does not itself mean a country can manage its internal conflicts more easily, if the government faces major economic problems whose alleviation requires long-term efforts, including major structural changes in the economy and society. The strength and cohesion, and ultimately the survival of different societies, depend on their ability to fulfil their basic promises. The success of democratic change in the CEE countries requires not just wise new leadership, good governance and popular support, but favourable social and economic conditions, at home and in the external environment. Greater prosperity will support the democratic process by enhancing social stability. The transition crises in the former socialist countries pointed to the need to search for new alternatives, but they also revealed the difficulties of creating a market system with a human face, in an era of globalization, without a clear national vision or commitment sustained by democratic coalitions, and without strong international support. I share the view of the American political scientist R.D. Kaplan:

Modern democracy exists within a thin band of social and economic conditions, which include flexible hierarchies that allow people to move up and down the ladder. Instead of clear-cut separations between classes there are many gray shades, with most people bunched in the middle. Democracy is fraud in many poor countries outside this narrow band ...[18]

Several decades must go by before the fate of this region is known. Will it become a Europeanized, democratic network of friendly states, with frontiers open to the free flow of goods, capital, expertise, technology, and labour, and an acceptable standard of living for the vast majority of its people, or will it become a region of poverty, turmoil, governed by new autocratic regimes helped to power by various forces, separated from the mainstream of the democratic societies not by the Iron Curtain of old, but by a new, "golden curtain" drawn by the West?

Notes

1. Naturally there were important differences between the CEE countries before the Second World War. Some had democratic institutions before the German occupation (Czechoslovakia, and to a certain extent Hungary and Romania), while others had no democratic traditions at all. However, even the latter offered the minimum political and legal conditions for a market system to function: transparent property rights, effective enforcement of contracts and other legal undertakings, and legal equality among economic agents. (There was, of course, a record of political extremism in the region, the darkest chapter of which was the Holocaust.)
2. The communist regimes eliminated private entrepreneurship and the main legal conditions for a market system, while introducing a political system centred around one-party rule.
3. The change to the socialist system some decades ago played a crucial role in determining the participation of China and Vietnam in the global economy. They developed institutions and policies that resembled those of the European socialist countries in many ways. These included state-controlled trading, the subordination of external economic relations to national priorities and plans, and the separation of prices and exchange rates from global market trends. However, there were also some important differences, especially in China's case, which developed several original patterns in its international economic relations and in some areas showed greater flexibility than the Soviet Union. After the Sino-Soviet split, China no longer suffered the same "strategic" constraints on technology imports from the West as did Soviet-bloc countries.
4. For more detail, see Simai, Mihály (1990), *Global Power Structure, Technology and the World Economy in the Late Twentieth Century*, London: Pinter Publishers, and Budapest: Akadémiai, pp. 61–108.
5. In my interpretation, a socio-economic system is defined by the character and development of its institutions, patterns, and forms of ownership, and the incentives and sources of information for its main economic actors.
6. There are different sources of strength, and of fragility and weakness, in the different political systems, and in the political systems of individual countries. The former etatist-socialist regimes of Central and Eastern Europe legitimized their political system to a large extent by promising economic achievements and a constant improvement in the standard of living. It was becoming increasingly evident by the 1970s that they could not keep their promises, or even sustain the levels already achieved. Stagnation and decline in the standard of living and in-

tensification of domestic political conflict resulted from the strains imposed by the arms race, by external economic difficulties, particularly the oil-price explosion, and by deteriorating economic performance. Another important factor was change in the Soviet Union. There had been popular uprisings in East Germany in 1953 and Hungary in 1956. The Prague Spring of 1968 was also an effort to introduce systemic changes. These attempts had been crushed by Soviet forces, at times when the domestic political structure of the Soviet Union was still relatively stable. By the end of the 1980s, Soviet domestic political stability had also been eroded by the external and internal political and economic conflicts, persistent economic stagnation, and declining standards of living. The reforms of Gorbachev also brought important changes in Soviet policies. By the end of the 1980s, the Soviet Union was neither willing nor able to use its earlier methods of crushing mass movements and "velvet revolutions" in CEE countries. The events that ended in the collapse of the Soviet Union in 1992 had gained an irresistible momentum.

7. Thurow, Lester C. (1996), *The Future of Capitalism*, London: Penguin Books, p. 242.
8. See, for instance, Kaplan, R.D. (1997), "Was Democracy Just a Moment?" *The Atlantic Monthly*, Vol. 280, No. 6, p. 55.
9. Naisbitt, John (1995), *Global Paradox*, New York: Avon Books, p. 25.
10. Naisbitt (1995), p. 47.
11. Kozul-Wright, Richard, and Paul Rayment (1995), *Walking on Two Legs: Strengthening Democracy and Productive Entrepreneurship in the Transition Economies*, Discussion Papers No. 101, New York: UNCTAD, p. 15.
12. The existence of an appropriate legal framework is a necessary, but not always sufficient condition for sustaining democracy. The role of the constitution, the law, institutions, and policies, legitimized by broad-based bodies and standards of legal cultivation, need to develop in harmony. Several countries have a remarkably low standard of legal culture, in the bureaucracy and society at large. The institutions of democracy in most are riddled with inconsistencies and imprecise legal formulae. The electoral systems introduced tend to be highly complex. In all countries in the region, there is an ongoing debate about changes in the electoral system, and the relative merits of proportional and majority representation. The argument for the latter rests on a probably misplaced hope that it will combat political fragmentation and promote coalescence into a stable two or three-party system. Proportional representation (in some cases with thresholds to eliminate parties with low support) is recommended as a way to stimulate the development and consolidation of political parties. The result in most countries is a compromise, an eclectic system that combines the two principles, but the compromise still attracts criticism and the debate continues. In general the problem really lies elsewhere. Experience in Western Europe shows that no electoral system can work well until there are modern political parties with relatively stable constituencies supporting them.
13. See *Transition: The Newsletter about Reforming Economies* (1994), The World Bank, April, Vol. 5, No. 4, p. 6.
14. The new legal and regulatory framework had to ease or liberalize market-entry procedures, rights to establish firms, and repatriation of profits and capital investments. It had to deal with the taxation of foreign investment (including

agreements on double taxation), the ownership of land, currency conversion, protection of intellectual property rights, and other aspects like conditions of acquisition. Another set of necessary regulatory measures related to accounting practices. In some countries, such as Russia, there was a piecemeal approach to developing the framework required, while in others, like Hungary, there was a more comprehensive approach.

15. Moreover there are several FDI-related multilateral agreements which the ex-socialist countries have joined or wish to do so, e.g. the World Trade Organization's TRIM and arbitration system and provisions on protecting intellectual property rights, and the Multilateral Investment Guarantee Agreement (MIGA).

16. Their economic power has also been weakened by economic collapse on a scale unprecedented in peacetime. One of the obvious consequences of the problems encountered by the European transition countries has been the decline in GDP. The accumulated loss of GDP by these countries in 1990–1995, about US$ 1,400 billion, exceeded their total output in 1989. Industrial and agricultural output declined fast, due to the collapse of Eastern markets, the shortage or loss of funds, which made important inputs unaffordable, the crowding-out effect of imports, and the shrinking domestic purchasing power. The loss of output and income was greater and more persistent than in the US and Germany in the Great Depression of the 1930s. A disturbing factor has been the high human cost of the changes. Regional figures for unemployment do not reliably reflect the decline in employment. In Russia, for instance, workers are retained on very low wages, even if a factory's capacity utilization falls below 50 per cent. The worsening employment situation and downgrading of skills are major features in all these countries. The outcome for the public appears not only in declining standards of living, but in greater social insecurity, higher unemployment, and long-term poverty.

17. The American scholar J.T. Johnson put the question like this: "Is liberal democratic self-government, in the form it has taken in the West, capable of being developed also in societies whose traditions and cultures are different from those of the Western democracies?" His answer is that "even though this achievement is historically and culturally tied to certain particular societies and their intellectual and social histories, such democracy may also 'travel' across historical and cultural lines to become the basis of political life in other societies." See Johnson, James Turner (1992), "Does Democracy Travel? Some Thoughts on Democracy and Its Cultural Context," *Ethics in International Affairs*, Vol. 6, pp. 41–55.

18. Kaplan (1997), p. 80.

3

Establishment of an independent, neutral civil service in the former socialist countries of Central and Eastern Europe

György Jenei

Governance and political democracy have become a key issue in the transition process and in modernization. This amounts to a shift in the paradigm for the administrative reforms that are taking place. The twentieth century displayed a seemingly irreconcilable dichotomy between *legalism* and *managerialism*, but since the 1980s, there have been fundamental changes in public administration, brought about by applying the management methods of private business. These have been coupled with a general effort to reduce the scope of the welfare state.

This has created a new situation. The economic, political, and social pressure on public administration has increased, forcing the bureaucracy to consider the requirements of legalism and managerialism concurrently. This has caused tensions and uncertainties in both the science and the practice of public administration in democratic countries. The salient trend in modern public administration is the pursuit of greater operational *efficiency* and *effectiveness*. Often the desire to achieve this tempts officials to depart from the tried, legitimate processes and institutions in a way that threatens to weaken and even endanger the democratic processes.

Public administration faces many different pressures and challenges. Many people, for instance, are losing confidence in all kinds of public institutions, which themselves face pressures on their resources and budgets, because their existing commitments coincide with new demands. Meanwhile there are calls for more "direct" democracy and more opportunities for participation. These trends are accompanied by decreasing respect for the traditional instruments of "representative" democracy.

The traditional civil service was established to run in a stable and predictable way, in a relatively static environment. This meant it was resistant to change. Today's civil service, on the other hand, has to adjust and accommodate to a rapidly and sometimes unpredictably changing environment. Civil servants need managerial skills. They must not be inward-looking or averse to risk-taking. At the same time, the civil service needs to recognize political realities and be able to participate not only in the implementation of decisions but in policy-making. So there obviously has to be a reinterpretation of what kind of impartial, independent civil service is needed in the Western world.

In the Central and Eastern European (CEE) countries, the situation is more complicated still. The crucial issue in the region is not to redesign, but to *establish* an independent, neutral civil service. This has to be done while democratization continues, far-reaching changes occur in the role of government, and the market economy establishes itself. So this civil service must be professionally expert and at the same time transparent and democratically accountable. Furthermore, the transition countries have several specific problems that present often difficult and unmanageable tasks to the system of public administration and its civil servants. Some relate to religious, ethnic, and cultural diversity, others to the transition process. Two of the main sources of cultural difference are religion and language. Indeed, the deepest divide in the CEE region runs between the Orthodox faith and the Western Christian denominations (Roman Catholic, Reformed, Lutheran, Unitarian). Poland, for instance, has a strong Roman Catholic identity. Other countries in the region, such as Bosnia and Bulgaria, contain Moslem ethnic minorities. Hungary is heterogeneous in its religious affiliation, while there is an Orthodox-Greek Catholic divide running through Ukraine. Another great challenge is posed by the region's unresolved ethnic conflicts, which are more divisive than they are elsewhere in Europe. Indeed majority-minority conflicts are constant sources of crisis in the region, which cause political disruption and have the potential to blow society apart.

Another set of problems is caused by widespread impoverishment and mass unemployment, whose appearance has coincided with cuts in welfare services. These relate directly to the transition (and are often compounded by ethnic hatred). The difficult process of transforming a command economy into a market economy would be helped if citizens resigned themselves to not achieving a higher standard of living immediately, and enduring harder conditions, harder work, and fewer state benefits for a prolonged period. Without such a recognition by the public, the social basis for democracy will remain weak and fragile and the political system may prove unable to bear the strain. This presents a danger of a populist, charismatic leader appearing, who appeals to those dissatisfied with the fruits of the transition. It is especially hard for society to accept greater burdens if the majority see a minority of the public making conspicuous gains by the changes, while the other groups are losers. There is wide and increasing socio-economic differentiation within and between the CEE countries. In the region's more advanced countries, inflation was curbed sooner and the falls in GDP and fiscal revenue were smaller than in the intermediate or latecomer groups (see Table 3.1), and the commitment to political democracy seems to be stronger.

These circumstances, coupled with the tasks of *institution and market-building*, place extraordinary pressure on the management and workforce in the public sector. There is also a pressure to reduce public-sector spending, due to chronic deficits and to calls from the general public for lower taxes and less official extravagance. On the other hand, citizens call for more and better public services, while private-sector business wants to see an improved infrastructure and additional services to facilitate international competitiveness.

Historical patterns and current tasks

Reform of the bureaucracy in the former socialist countries forms part of the economic and political transition. What can be learnt in this respect from the various transitions that have occurred in market capitalism?

Historically, there have been two types of systemic transition to a market economy. The first is the market-led, evolutionary, "organic" type followed by Britain, the first industrial nation, and later by the United States, France, the Netherlands, Belgium, and the Scandinavian countries. In this type of transition the state did not play a dominant role, it merely facilitated the development. The second is a functional, state-led transition in which the role of the state is decisive, especially in the beginning.

Table 3.1 **Progress with the transition and macroeconomic performance (measured by the median of each group)**

Countries	Private sector's share of GDP (%)[a]	Score for enterprise restructuring, privatization[a]	Score for liberalization of markets[a]	Score for banking reform[a]	Score for investment laws[a]	Government fiscal balance, 1995 (% of GDP)[a]	Cumulative fall in fiscal revenues, 1989–93 (% of GDP)[b]	Annual inflation rate (%)		Ratio of lowest recorded GDP to GDP in 1989[b]	GDP growth, 1955 (%)[a]	Increase in infant mortality rate (%)[c]
								1992	1995			
Advanced transition	60	3.7	3.3	3	3	−1	−5	93	22	76	5	−15
Intermediate transition	42	2.7	2.8	2	2	−7	−20	237	28	65	0	7
Early transition	27	2	2.3	1.8	2	−4	−18	1,364	125	49	−5	15.6

Notes: The sources are as follows: *a. Transition Report 1995,* London: EBRD, pp. 11 and 185–186. The qualitative indicators of reform in columns 2–6 range from 1 to 4*, classed as 5 when medians were calculated. Most advanced industrial economies would qualify for a 4* rating for almost all these indicators. 1 indicates a negligible change from the old position. *b.* IMF Finance Statistics and World Development Report (1997), *The State in a Changing World,* Oxford University Press, for the World Bank. *c. Crisis in Mortality, Health and Nutrition,* New York: UNICEF, p. 6. *d.* Projection: this excludes quasi-fiscal central-bank deficits. Cash balances are used where other fiscal figures are not available. Data for Tajikistan, Belarus, and Turkmenistan were not available. The groups are as follows: advanced – Croatia, Czech Republic, Estonia, Hungary, Latvia, Lithuania, Latvia, Poland, Slovakia, Slovenia; intermediate – Albania, Bulgaria, FYR Macedonia, Kyrgyzstan, Romania, Russian Federation; early – Armenia, Azerbaijan, Belarus, Georgia, Kazakhstan, Moldova, Tajikistan, Turkmenistan, Ukraine, Uzbekistan. The table is taken from Buiter, Willem, Ricardo Lago, and Nicholas Stern (1997), *Promoting an Effective Market Economy in a Changing World,* EBRD Working Paper No. 23, April, London: European Bank for Reconstruction and Development, pp. 14–15.

There were several interesting examples of the functional type of transition during the nineteenth and twentieth centuries. Probably the best known were Russia's in the second half of the nineteenth century, during the reign of Tsar Alexander II, and the Meiji restoration in Japan. The role of bureaucrats strongly committed to modernization and the national interest was decisive in those countries. For example, Sergei Witte, as finance minister and one of the leading Tsarist policy-makers, tried in a memorandum to persuade Nicholas II to undertake a transition programme in spite of the foreseeable sacrifices:

International competition does not wait. If we do not take energetic and de-cisive measures ... the rapidly growing foreign industries will break through our tariff barriers and establish themselves in our fatherland ... and drive their roots into the depths of our economy. This may gradually clear the way also for triumphant political penetration by foreign powers ... Our economic backwardness may lead to political and cultural backwardness as well.[1]

Witte was an enlightened, extremely vigorous personality, but his influence depended upon the Tsar, so that he was not an independent or neutral civil servant. However, he had relative autonomy based on his expertise and strong commitment to modernization. There were also strong personalities, similar to Witte, in the Japanese civil service. Among them was Masayoshi Matsukata, the minister of finance, an extraordinarily able personality who successfully introduced a severe deflationary policy at the beginning of the 1880s.

The beginning of the transition was essentially identical in Japan and Tsarist Russia. Both suffered a similar initial shock, followed by several years of confusion, but in the third and fourth decades of the process, important differences emerged. The Russian reform pro-ceeded unevenly, and was only completed in 1906–1911 by P.A. Stolypin. It was constrained by military defeat at the hands of Japan and by serious peasant uprisings. As W.E. Mosse puts it,

Everywhere the institutions of Nicholas continued to exist side by side with those of the reforming age. The Ministry of the Interior, controlling the all-important provincial Governors, whose power was undiminished, remained in the hands of bureaucratic centralizers ... At every step there was unre-solved conflict between the new and the old.[2]

During the same period, the Japanese transition was occurring gradually, without ambiguity of that sort. The difference was because the introduction of a market economy in Japan came after the politi-cal transformation, while in Russia it was undertaken by the *ancien régime*.[3]

Under the slogan *fukoku-kyohei* (enrich the country, strengthen the army), Japan established a totally new political framework. The changes included unifying the structure and administration of government, establishing legal equality for all social classes and property rights in land, and eliminating restrictions in various spheres, including freedom of movement and internal trade, choice of crops grown, and entry into new occupations. Other important changes affected the armed forces, education, the law, and the police.[4] The reforms evidently promoted liberalism and democratization.

Comparing the process in Russia and Japan leads to the conclusion that in the initial phase of economic transition, democracy is not a prior requirement for establishing a market economy. However, the absence of democracy causes delay, ambiguity, and volatility during the transition.

The current transition in the CEE countries is clearly not of the organic type. The state assists the private sector in many ways. It creates the overall legal and economic framework for the transition and serves as a major economic agent. The development of an independent, neutral civil service is a key component of the transition in all its main dimensions – from totalitarianism to democracy, from a command economy to a market system, from state to private ownership, and from a bloc structure to national independence. The civil service also has the additional task of helping to improve performance and stimulate society's commitment to the key tasks. Professional expertise gains crucial importance when society is under various pressures, facing difficult tasks and challenges. Without providing it, the civil service cannot serve the long-term interests of society. Instead it will merely react to the strongest pressures put upon it, without embodying any real commitment.

There are three levels of state institutions; national, regional, and local. The degree of autonomy at the regional and local levels is crucial because of its influence on implementation processes. Under a democratic political system, local institutions have significant autonomy and are therefore subject to various political influences. Interest groups have real opportunities to influence political decisions and policy implementation.

The state traditionally performs certain fundamental functions, among the more important being the maintenance of law and order, and of peace, in other words of internal and external security. All political systems employ police and armed forces to guarantee their internal and external security. The state also has an important role in protecting property rights and providing a system of civil law to adjudicate between citizens. The role of the state in the CEE countries became extended in the twentieth century, with an accompanying growth of government bureaucracy. The etatist, state-socialist state took direct control over a wide area of economic and social activity not included in the state's traditional functions. This has been profoundly affected by the transition to a market system. In some areas there is a degree of continuity, while in others there have been important changes in response to new requirements. A typical example of such continuity and change is the welfare function, including education, public health, pensions, social allowances, and housing. More important changes are taking place in the economic functions of the state, particularly in monetary and fiscal policy and redistributive objectives and instruments. Another important area includes regulatory activities to limit the adverse impact of behaviour: environmental protection, consumer protection, curbs on monopolies and cartels, and so on, where the importance of the state may be increasing. All these fields require major institutional and administrative reforms, and substantial changes in the role, composition, size, working methods, and quality of performance of the government bureaucracy.

The most important elements of public sector reform include:
– privatization programmes, including contracting out processes;
– decentralization of decision-making to the regional and local levels, to provide genuine legal and financial autonomy for local institutions;
– deregulation and transparency;
– transforming and flattening out public organizations, so that they are not only reactive, but proactive in connection with changes in public requirements and remands, as well as being less expensive to run;
– changing procurement policy, financial and human-resource management, and information systems in public organizations, so that government agencies can work more effectively towards new forms of cooperation with non-governmental organizations and the private sector, and give more attention to the citizens they serve;
– measuring the performance and outcome of public-sector activities by reviewing and monitoring, rather than commanding and controlling.

It is also important for the bureaucracies to sustain institutional stability and predictability, while keeping up with the changes. This presents major challenges for management and the staff of government agencies. Civil servants need new technical skills and new types of attitudes and values, but they must also preserve their traditional strengths.

Independent, neutral civil servants or policy-making bureaucrats?

The emergence of a modern bureaucracy and the transition to democracy raise an old question. What role should the technically qualified, expert administration play? Should it confine itself to "neutral" administrative tasks or also be active in the policy-making process?

The increasing importance of the bureaucracy results from the growing complexity of the modern economic and political system. These trends were already evident at the end of the last century. The most influential explanation of them has been Max Weber's. Weber's theory of bureaucracy was associated with his analysis of the basic types of authority, of which he identified three: charismatic, traditional, and rational-legal. Charismatic authority was based on "devotion to the specific and exceptional sanctity, heroism or exemplary character of an individual person."[5] The weakness of charismatic authority is that it is unstable, due to the personal nature of the relationship between leader and followers, which makes the development of permanent institutions difficult. Traditional authority can be characterized as "an established belief in the sanctity of immemorial traditions and the legitimacy of the status of those exercising authority under them."[6] The weakness of traditional authority is its static nature.

Compared with charismatic authority or traditional authority, rational-legal authority is based on "a belief in the legality of patterns of normative rules, and the right of those elevated to authority under such rules to issue commands."[7] The development of rational-legal authority is connected to the evolution of modern industrialized society. It is generally recognized that this type of authority is superior to the other two types, because it meets higher performance standards in rational administrative settings.

Contemporary politics, Weber claimed, was shaped first, by the emergence of modern bureaucracy, especially the growing state apparatus, which was increasingly led by technically trained, professional career administrators. The second trend that Weber observed was somewhat oblique to the first: the rise of a new class of professional politicians whose influence was based not on inherited social status, but on mass political parties claiming the membership and suffrage of millions of ordinary citizens. Almost a century later, Weber's insights seem remarkably prescient. Every society of any size needs a bureaucracy. Not all social interaction can be managed by altruism, anarchy, or markets.

The public sector has to provide public goods and services in response to citizens' legitimate needs and problems. This normative imperative is one of the most commonly accepted foundations of modern societies. The development of the public sector can be seen as a process of bureaucratization. The employees of the public sector, government offices, and administrative agencies have important roles in public decision-making. They are bureaucrats – the technical term for government officials and employees – who in an early social climate were referred to more kindly as civil servants.

Bureaucrats conceptualize problems and prepare decision-making options for politicians. They also implement the decisions made by politicians (in parliament or in the government). There is a general trend in modern societies to increase rational bureaucratic authority, without which societies are unable to cope with the complex administration that is required.

The main features of the bureaucracy are these:
1. They act or work on a legal basis, so that their role is regulated by law and their office runs according to fixed rules.
2. There is a hierarchical pyramid of authority within the office.
3. Management of a modern office is based upon written documents.
4. Officers are specially trained and work full time at their jobs.

It is important to note that the word "bureaucrats" has at least two meanings. While most people in the bureaucracy carry out administrative tasks, a smaller, senior group is involved heavily in policy-making.

The perceived impartiality of the civil service is derived from these characteristics. The pattern of the division of labour between bureaucrats and politicians was described by Woodrow Wilson:

Administration lies outside the proper sphere of politics. Administrative questions are not political questions ... The field administration is a field of business. It is removed from the hurry and strife of politics ... it is a part of political life only as the methods of the counting-house are a part of the life of society; only as machinery is part of the manufactured product.[8]

Frank Goodnow had the same idea when he emphasized that the functions of the state have to be divided into the expression of the public will (politics) and the execution of that will (administration).

Although this division between politics and administration is now seen as outdated and naive by most public-administration scholars, it might have some lingering usefulness when attempting to modernize the civil service in the CEE countries. However, bureaucrats try to use their professional expertise not only to maintain their neutrality, but to influence the decision-making processes. This was pointed out clearly by Weber:

Under normal conditions, the power position of a fully developed bureaucracy is always overpowering. The "political master" finds himself in the position of a "dilettante" who stands opposite the "expert" facing the trained official who stands within the management of administration.[9]

In this century, civil services have become central actors in the government of post-industrial societies. So why, in democracies, has this trend not led to an authoritarian system run by a central bureaucratic state? This is because of the strength of civil society – the strength of pressure groups and the well-functioning articulation of interests by various social groups.

In the socialist, etatist regimes of Central and Eastern Europe there were "technocrats" and "experts" working in the apparatus. Some groups among them tried to initiate reforms in the centrally planned economy, because they had a stronger commitment to modernization. These reforms were in the main blocked or aborted by the political system. Hungary was an exceptional case in many respects, but even here the reform remained partial and limited. Full implementation would have required a pluralistic reform of the whole political system. Technocrats were able to help in sustaining certain efforts towards reform, but they could not establish the necessary social and political foundations for radical change. However, even its partial reforms gave Hungary an advantage in 1989, in the beginning of the transition. The political and economic reforms in the years leading up to the change of system facilitated a smoother, peaceful transition and relatively rapid establishment of the legal and political framework for a liberal, democratic system.

The creation of a new bureaucracy in Hungary: Trends and problems

One of the most daunting challenges of the economic and political transition in Hungary has been to reform the civil service and modernize the bureaucratic system.

The first important step was constitutional reform, to guarantee civil and political rights, freedom of the press and the right to association, and to lay the foundations of a pluralistic political system. Parallel with this political reform, there had to be a basic reform of the institutional system of the public administration. Multi-party democracy and a market economy had quite different requirements from the previous system. In the process of modernizing the public sector, the Hungarian government enacted important pieces of legislation integral to the transition to a market-oriented society. The government made great efforts to build up a new environment through changes in the systems of institutions and types of ownership. To achieve these basic goals, about 70 new pieces of legislation had to be passed. Modernization of the public sector was one of the key fields involved.

Act XXIII/1992 (1 July) covers the legal status of civil servants. This supplies the necessary provisions for establishing a politically neutral, impartial civil service, operating on a legal foundation. The act emphasizes the need for public servants to have the requisite professional skills. The agenda was set by Government Resolution No. 1026/1992 (12 May) on modernization of public administration, which entrusted various ministries with the reform process.

Act XXXVII/1992 (19 June) lays down the control and management system of public administration. The act was implemented by Government Resolutions 137–40/1993 (10 December) in the following fields:

– the system of planning, management, and control of public institutions;
– the responsibility of subsystems in public administration for planning, reporting, and record-keeping;
– certain questions relating to implementation of the central state budget;
– methods for subsystems of state administration to cover bank accountancy, deposit management, the money supply, and payables;
– the system of planning and financing governmental investments.

The act and the resolutions, together with the act on the annual central state budget, regulate the whole process of management of public institutions. These reforms brought changes in the main characteristics of the Hungarian bureaucracy.

The Hungarian bureaucracy has been reduced in size, although several new agencies have been established. Its gender structure has shifted in favour of women. There were 3,065 public-institution units on 31 March 1997, which was 75 less than in 1995, due mainly to a fall in the number at regional level (from 410 to 340 units), clearly as a result of modernization efforts in public management. On the same date there were 104,646 officials working in the public administration – 2.8 per cent less than in 1996 (107,699) and 3.5 per cent less than in 1993 (108,386). However, this was not a simple decrease. Several new public institutions were created between 1993 and 1997, the main ones being the National Tax Office, the Institute of Telecommunications and Management, the State Property Agency, the State Asset Holding Company, the Office for National and Ethnic Minorities, and the Office for Environment Protection. So the aggregate decrease in the number of public officials includes increments in several parts of the bureaucracy.[10]

The quality and composition of the bureaucracy in modern societies have an important influence on many areas, influencing not only the implementation of political decisions, but often the content of them as well. Lipsky's theory of the role of street-level (*i.e.* local-level) bureaucrats gained considerable influence in the 1980s. He argued that policies are reshaped by bureaucrats at the local level. This means "the decisions of street-level bureaucrats, the routines they establish, and the devices they invent to cope with uncertainties and work pressure, effectively become the public policies they carry out."[11]

Bureaucracies are complex structures that make a wide variety of demands on individual officials. The public often hold negative views of bureaucrats, perceiving them as rigid and slow and productive of "red tape," but there are positive perceptions of them as well, as independent actors trapped within the bureaucratic organization. Another common picture of bureaucrats is of individuals obsessed with the intricate rules they must follow. People often enter public employment with some commitment to service, but that is weakened by the conditions under which they work and the expectations of the public they serve. Lipsky argues that "the very nature of this work prevents them from coming close to the ideal conception of their jobs. Large classes or huge caseloads and inadequate resources combine with the uncertainties of method and the unpredictability of clients to defeat their aspirations as service workers."[12]

Hungary and the other CEE countries require a new type of civil servant, who can be paternalistic or protective as required, but can also work as a partner and an efficient manager, and who possesses

71

personal integrity and independence from the political process. There are also some increasingly important technical skills required, especially with the information revolution.

There have been some other changes in the structure of the Hungarian bureaucracy besides the gender shift already mentioned. The proportion working in central government has increased. Larger numbers of highly educated people have moved into civil-service positions, causing some qualitative improvement. However, transforming the structure of any bureaucracy is a long and difficult process.

It is difficult to say whether officials are more independent and neutral than they were at the beginning of the 1990s. The strategic objectives of the reform and the main trends in implementing it were unaffected by the change in the government's political complexion after the 1994 general election. Another positive sign has been the preservation of a distinction between political appointees in public administration and professional career staff. This means that growing importance is attached to independence, although the implementation process is slow in some respects. The delays are partly due to lack of expertise and a bureaucratic attitude, but partly to the complexity of the process.

Improving the professional qualifications of civil servants is an important goal in Hungarian public administration. Recruits now have to receive training in the functioning of a modern state and the system of public administration, as well as learning their field of specialization. They are examined on these.

Another crucial issue is whether the ongoing reforms should focus on greater autonomy, on business-like managerialism, or on the ethical requirements of day-to-day work in public administration. Even in the developed Western countries, there is anxiety that giving the bureaucracy broader responsibility may threaten or weaken the legal state (*Rechtstaat*). The growing autonomy of bureaucrats and the expansion of business-like managerialism may damage the integrity of civil servants and the ethical foundations of the public sector. Obviously the danger of this and the ensuing damage will be greater in the CEE countries, where the legal state and constitutionalism lack strong historical traditions and political systems have generally been oppressive. The ethical damage has been very serious in the region because there was no legal transparency in public administration.

A further problem is the hiatus or vacuum of values during the transition. There are no ethical standards for bureaucrats, sanctioned

Index of corruption

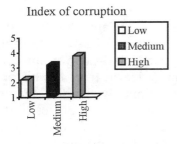

Policy distortion index

Index of corruption

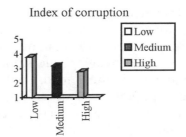

Predictability of judiciary index

Index of corruption

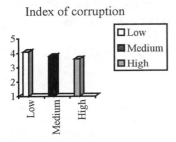

Merit-based recruitment

Index of corruption

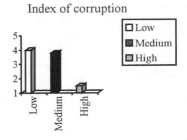

Ratio of civil service wages to manu-
facturing wages

Note: Each index score is the average for a group of countries. Higher values of the corruption index mean more corruption, and similarly for the other variables. The top left-hand panel is based on a simple correlation for 39 industrial and developing countries during 1984-1993 (for the policy distortion index) and 1996 (for the corruption index). The top right panel is based on a regression using data from 59 industrial and developing countries during 1996. The bottom left-hand panel is based on a regression using data for 35 developing countries during 1970-1990. The bottom right-hand panel is based on a simple correlation for 20 industrial and developing countries in the late 1980s to early 1990s; wage data are means. *Source:* World Bank staff calculations. Published in *The State in a Changing World*, for the World Bank, Oxford: Oxford University Press, 1997, p. 8.

Fig. 3.1 **Factors associated with corruption**

by a democratic, consensus-based process. Corruption, for instance, a clear indicator of the ethical integrity of civil servants, has become one of the big obstacles to improving the effectiveness of the public sector and reinvigorating state institutions in the region. It has various sources and motivating factors. Some of them, discussed in detail in the World Development Report of the World Bank, certainly apply to the CEE countries (see Fig. 3.1).

In conclusion, reform of the civil service has critical importance in all areas of the transition process. It relates especially closely to democratization and economic reform in Central and Eastern Europe, where the changing role of the state has particularly important consequences in those fields. While much can be learnt from the historical experiences of other transitions, the ultimately decisive factors will be the cultural, social, economic, and institutional features of the former socialist countries themselves. There are several key components of the reform that must be carried out. The most important are the assurance of political integrity, autonomy, and transparency, and qualitative improvements in effectiveness and in ethical and moral attitudes. The development of a new civil service will be a long-term, continuing process in all CEE countries, of which only the first steps have so far been taken.

Notes

1. Von Laue, T.H. (1963), *Sergei Witte and the Industrialisation of Russia*, p. 3. Cited by Feinstein, Charles (1990), *Historical Precedents for Economic Change in Central Europe and the USSR*, Boston: Credit Suisse First Boston, and Oxford: Oxford Analytica, p. 7.
2. Mosse, W.H. (1965), *Alexander II and the Industrialization of Russia*, revised edition, p. 89. Cited by Feinstein (1990).
3. Feinstein (1990), p. 10.
4. Ibid.
5. Weber, Max (1947), *The Theory of Social and Economic Organization*, translated by A.M. Henderson and T. Parsons, Glencoe, Ill.: Free Press, p. 328.
6. Ibid.
7. Ibid.
8. Wilson, Woodrow (1887), "The Study of Administration," *Political Sciences Quarterly*, No. 2 (June), pp. 209–210. Cited by Shafritz, Jay M., and Albert C. Hyde, eds. (1992), *Classics of Public Administration*, 3rd edition, Belmont, Calif.: Brooks-Cole Publishing Co., p. 18.
9. Cited by Diamant, Alfred (1963), "The Bureaucratic Model: Max Weber Rejected, Rediscovered, Reformed," in Ferrel Heady and Sybil L. Stokes (eds.), *Papers in Comparative Public Administration*, Ann Arbor: University of Michigan, Institute of Public Adminstration, p. 85.
10. The new coalition government in Hungary which came into power after the elections in 1998 introduced certain changes in the institutional structure of government bureaucracy, which may be resulting in an increase in their staff again.
11. Lipsky, M. (1980), *Street-Level Bureaucracy*, New York: Russell Sage, p. xii.
12. Ibid.

Case studies

4

Interrelations between political and economic change in Russia and the CIS countries: A comparative analysis

Oleg Bogomolov

The political changes and economic transformation in the Russian Federation show many characteristics that differ from those of the Central and Eastern European countries, and of the other former Soviet republics. Although there is a direct connection between political transformation and transition to a market economy, as in all the post-socialist states, Russia's position as a world power and heir to most of the Soviet Union's economic potential, research capacity, and military might strongly influences the political process.

The sheer size of Russia makes democratization and marketization harder and more complex than in other countries. Another factor is its ethnic diversity. Then there is the role of the Russian Federation within the Commonwealth of Independent States (CIS), the loose cooperation framework of Soviet successor states. Some CIS members look on Russia as an essential partner. Others, though willing to continue cooperation, feel menaced by the possibility that the "empire" might be restored. Detailed analysis of these problems would go beyond the scope of this paper, but they are factors to consider when contemplating the political and economic issues of transition to a democratic market economy.[1] There is a strong interaction between the political and the economic factors and processes. Market reforms and consolidation of these require political commitment and support.

The development and consolidation of private ownership and market structures exert a strong influence on the political system, by promoting a civil society, democratizing the state system, and strengthening law and order. However, the Central and Eastern European (CEE) and the CIS countries differ markedly in the character of these interrelations and in the outcome of them.

As a result of the "velvet," virtually bloodless revolutions in the CEE countries, the collapse of the communist regime was followed by a new, still-changing system shaped by well-structured political forces. The impetus behind this anti-totalitarian, democratic transformation came from the reformist wings of the old ruling parties, the political dissidents, and the anti-system opposition, with mass support. The forces of change were opposed to the command economy and in agreement about dismantling the party-state system. Society chose democracy, a constitutional state, and respect for human rights, and has shown no signs of retreating from that choice.

The social transformation in the former Soviet Union, and later in Russia, took different lines. The gradual evolution of the communist system effected during Gorbachev's *perestroika* was halted by the coup attempt of a conservative section of the communist leadership, and the subsequent dissolution of the communist party and disintegration of the Soviet Union. Gorbachev's slow, excessively cautious reforms, designed to modernize the existing system, not cause radical change, led to discontent among the population. The economic situation was visibly worsening and something had to be urgently done about it. The public expected the Russian leaders who had shaken off the tutelage of the party centre to take immediate, resolute steps to reform the economy on market principles. Added to that there was the triumphant euphoria of the democratic forces after the defeat of the coup attempt, which aroused false hopes that radical reforms would bring rapid success. This explains why "shock therapy" was chosen. Furthermore, the policies of President Yeltsin were inclined towards short-term measures coupled with the use of force.

The hastily adopted economic policy line caused galloping inflation, sharp impoverishment of most citizens, a decline in production, unprecedented social differentiation, and rapid disillusionment among the political élite and the public. This led to a split in society and a stand-off between the legislature and the president. Events culminated in the autumn of 1993, in a tank fusillade against parliament, which was dissolved. There was a referendum resulting in a constitution tailored to an authoritarian ruler and a change in the nature of power. The competence of both chambers of the Federal Assembly (the State Duma and the Federation Council) was curtailed to a minimum. The head of state was invested with almost unlimited executive and legislative power, including supreme command of the armed forces. The Constitutional Court was also reformed: the number of judges serving on it was increased, which made it less independent of political opinion.

The new period of political development that began at the end of 1993 has brought a polarization of political forces. The radical democrats, having taken almost unlimited power, began to squeeze consumption, restrict budget spending, tighten the money and credit supply, and raise taxes, with the support of Western governments and the international financial institutions. This, however, failed to produce an improvement in the overall economic situation or a halt in the decline of production. There was a clear political presence of radical-liberal extremism, which provoked a build-up of forces and influence at the other pole, among the neo-communists and "national patriots." The Russian crisis in 1998 revealed all the problems of the political and of the economic system. The crisis in Russia has often been characterized as a purely financial crisis. This view was based on the assumption that the market transformation of the Russian economy has been largely successful. In fact, the situation was more complex. The Russian economy was suffering from a financial crisis at least from the beginning of autumn 1997 and this crisis entered its most acute phase in August 1998. The main components of this crisis were the permanent budget deficit and a resultant government debt crisis, the crisis of the banking system mainly linked to imbalances between foreign exchange liabilities and assets, a significant portion of investments in GKO on bank balance-sheets, and the foreign exchange crisis, which made it clear how dependent was the modern Russian economy upon the in- and outflows of foreign short-term capital and how important the US dollar was in Russia. There was however another, deeper factor in these crises: the constantly deteriorating financial position of the real sector of the economy. This was also related to the financial crisis. The "non-payments" by the state determined to a great extent the problems of the real sector. There is another paradox in the Russian system; the quasi (or pseudo) market nature of the economic system. Nearly all market institutions can be found in the Russian economy. There is a two-tier banking system, all major kinds of financial and trade intermediaries, stock and foreign exchange markets. All this creates an impression of a full-fledged market economy. This market infrastructure is little more than "Potiomkin's village," that is, it consists of some forms which are to a very significant degree deprived of their traditional content. Such a situation was an objective consequence of the deeply erroneous design of the market transformation of the Russian economy.

The outcome of marketization

"Shock therapy" was the method chosen by the region's reformers as a shortcut to macroeconomic stabilization and a market economy. The prices of most goods and domestic and foreign trade were liberalized all at once, before any competitive environment or elementary market infrastructure had emerged. This abrupt liberalization led inevitably to an inflationary spiral. The emphasis in combating this was placed on monetary and financial instruments, even though not all the factors contributing to the inflation were monetary. There was a belief that it would be senseless to take measures to stimulate industrial investment, reduce taxes, or harness idle capacity by expanding demand until the rate of inflation had been reduced to an acceptable 10–12 per cent.

The privatization of state assets took on a peculiar character. The state began shedding its most profitable enterprises and even whole industries, selling them at nominal prices to loyal members of the old and new *nomenklatura*. It is especially sad that such privatization did not usually promote modernization or reorganization of the corporate structure. The main reasonable justification for privatization – greater economic efficiency – was disregarded by the outside advisers and domestic authorities responsible for the reforms.

Market relations and market institutions which have developed in Russia have also resulted in a number of favourable changes. Goods shortages have disappeared. A new class of entrepreneurs started emerging. There were, however, several adverse trends in the first six years, even before the 1998 crisis. An unprecedented decline in the volume of production (with GDP halved, see Table 4.1) was accompanied by a degradation of production structure, a squandering of the technological core of a modern economy, and a drastic impoverishment of most of the population. Since the pre-reform level of 1991, investment has shrunk to 30 per cent in Belarus, 11 per cent in Kazakhstan, 20 per cent in Georgia, and 25 per cent in Ukraine. Russia has lost its earlier economic might. It now has a GDP lower than Mexico's, Brazil's or Indonesia's, only a fifth of the size of

Table 4.1 **Trends in GDP (percentage increases over the previous year)**

Country	1991	1992	1993	1994	1995	1996	1997 (forecast)	1996/ 1991 (%)
Russia	12.8	−19	−12	−15	−4.2	−6.0	−2.0–0	48
Ukraine	−10	−13.7	−14.2	−19	−11.8	−10.0	−5.0**	43
Belarus	−1.2	−9.6	−9.5	−20	−10	2.6	10.5**	60
Kazakhstan	−11.8	−13	−12.9	−25	−9	1.1	–	46
Uzbekistan	−0.5	−11.1	−2.4	−4	10	1.6	–	83
Turkmenistan	−5	−9.6	−10	−20	−10	0	–	56
Kyrgyzstan	−5	−16.4	−16.4	−26	−6	5.6	19.2***	49
Azerbaijan	−0.7	−22.6	−23.1	−22	−17	10	5.0**	39
Moldova	−18	−28.3	−4.8	−30	−3	−8	−4.3**	36

Notes:
  * 1995 as a percentage of 1990.
 ** January–September 1997 to January–September 1996.
*** January 1997 to January–September 1996.
Source: Vienna Institute for Comparative Economic Studies, Research Reports No. 239, 1997, p. 2.

China's, and less than a tenth of the size of the American GDP. Capital flight in the reform years is estimated to have exceeded US$ 100 billion. Domestic and foreign debt is rapidly rising: already it is equivalent to 60 per cent of annual GDP.

Household consumption in Russia has dropped to 40 per cent of its 1991 level, turning the clock back by 20 years in this respect. Widespread poverty has spread across the country. The official breadline is not a poverty line but the brink of destitution. Without reliable figures, it is impossible to verify what proportion of the population lives below it. Some estimates put it at 40 per cent. This impoverishment has been accompanied by a sharp polarization of incomes, which is a strong inhibitive factor to the economy. The income differentiation between the highest and lowest deciles is 15–20 times.

There has been a rapid worsening of the demographic situation. Russia's population has been declining for several years. Life expectancy at birth has fallen by four years, to only 58 for men. Rates of suicide and mental illness have soared. The numbers of beggars and homeless are rising. The ways and habits of pauperism are spreading to ever wider strata of Russian society, disrupting the moral principles of the state and the private lives of individuals. Organized crime, prospering at all levels in society, lays serious claim to extensive control over various sectors of the economy, politics, and law en-

Table 4.2 **Trends in consumer prices (percentage increases over the previous year)**

Country	1991	1992	1993	1994	1995	1996	1997 (forecast)	1996/1991 (%)
Russia	100.3	1,470	880	215	131	21.8	19	2,720**
Ukraine	94.4	1,650	9,260*	400*	380	39.7	37	117,013
Belarus	98.6	970	1,190	2,220	710	52.7	51	78,665
Kazakhstan	114.5	1,510	1,660	1,880	180	39.3	–	46,941
Uzbekistan	97.3	410	1,230	1,550	320	80	–	16,692
Turkmenistan	112.4	770	1,630	2,710	1,100	800	–	970,164
Azerbaijan	86.5	940	1,110	4,780	410	19.9	–	70,034
Moldova	114.4	1,110	1,180	490	30.0	24.0	–	3,158

Notes:
* December to December.
** The authenticity of the index is not confirmed by the rise in basic consumer-goods prices, which have multiplied 10,000–20,000 times over.
Source: As Table 4.1.

forcement. Culture, education, health care, and science are in deep trouble.

Further factual evidence is required to back the official arguments that the decline of GDP halted and recovery began in 1997. The conditions for stable growth and higher efficiency of the economy, particularly an increase in investment in fixed assets and the infrastructure and a resumption of growth in personal incomes, still have to be met.

One development cited as proof that the tide has turned is the sharp fall in the inflation rate (see Table 4.2). According to many Russian economists, the slowing of inflation, from 130 per cent in 1995 to 22 per cent in 1996 and about 14 per cent in 1997, was mainly due to massive arrears and non-payments between firms and to corporate indebtedness in general. By the beginning of 1997, the backlog of wage payments (48 trillion roubles – US$ 8.5 billion) and pension contributions (16 trillion roubles, US$ 3 billion) greatly exceeded the volume of the retail stock (38 trillion roubles). If the arrears owed to employees were paid, it could trigger a new surge of inflation. The state budget paid off some of its wage and salary liabilities at the end of 1997. The problem is not just the social tensions the situation causes. The settlement crisis, by disorganizing the economy and removing incentives for manufacturers and potential investors, itself becomes an obstacle to economic change.

The other CIS countries face similarly serious problems. Uzbekistan, Belarus and Azerbaijan took a more cautious, gradual approach than Russia to implementing market reforms, which meant they managed to stop the economic decline earlier. There is a sharp difference between the CIS countries and the CEE countries in this respect. The contraction of production in the CEE countries was relatively brief and not very deep (up to 20–25 per cent), so that economic growth returned by 1993-1994. The decline in the CIS countries has dragged on for several years. Not one of the CEE countries underwent the kind of slump in production and real personal incomes experienced in Russia, Ukraine, and several other CIS countries, where the reforms were accompanied by a surge of inflation.

The economies of Russia and the other CIS countries have suffered heavily from the collapse and almost complete rupture in the traditional economic ties and commercial exchanges between them, including industrial cooperation and mutual flows of capital and labour. The architects of Russia's market reforms assumed that Russia outside the Soviet Union would enhance its prospects of success in developing a market economy. Experience has shown this not to be so. Indeed a number of expert observers suggested that reinforcing economic ties within the former Soviet area could ease the market transition considerably and encourage the resumption of economic growth. Some steps were taken within the CIS framework to dismantle the rapidly emerging customs barriers between the new states, create a customs union, and found transnational companies. The Belarus leadership has gone furthest in promoting economic and political integration with Russia. However, economic reintegration poses delicate domestic and international political issues and is influenced by external powers. Pressures against the reintegration and restoration of the old ties come from local nationalists and from new foreign partners.

The political system and the role of the state

The Russian successors of the communist party differ from successor parties in the CEE countries. The latter have more or less become social democrats, rejecting basic communist tenets – violent revolution, one-party power, a non-market, command economy, predominant state ownership, and ideological control of society – in favour of social-democratic values and rational pragmatism. The mainstream among Russian communists is ideologically conservative and has not sloughed off its Bolshevik past. So their accession to power would have caused deep uncertainty and been unacceptable to much of the electorate.

The political process in Russia is evolving in a generally ambiguous and inconsistent way. One indisputable achievement is freedom of expression. There is no problem about registering a new party, organizing a rally or demonstration, convening a meeting, and so on. Citizens have the freedom to elect parliament and the president, local legislative bodies and governors, although the outcome of elections depends much on the stance of radio and television, which are effectively controlled by the authorities, and on the funds available to candidates. The ruling élite controls most of the financial resources. The system of political institutions is still being shaped by various forces. It lacks a clear division of responsibility between the legislature, executive, and judiciary. There is no system of checks and balances between these three divisions of power. The role and powers of Parliament on substantive issues have been minimized, and the power of presidency made decisive. Presidential decrees are extremely important. The law is often compromised and sacrificed for the benefit of the wealthy and influential. Political parties, with one or two exceptions, have little influence, because they are disorganized and too numerous. The political centre is especially weak. During election campaigns, the parties are in every respect subordinate to the state apparatus and the social organizations it controls.

These developments have given state power to a combination of the second and third echelons of the old party *nomenklatura*, the members of the liberal intelligentsia who have acquired political and/or financial capital, and the protégés of the emerging big financial and industrial interests. The six big financial and industrial groups, plus two other giant concerns – Gasprom and Lukoil – control more than 50 per cent of Russia's economic assets. Politically inexperienced and impatient, the new Russian tycoons are openly demanding an "appropriate" share in the policy-making, and control influential television channels and newspapers that can press their claims. Most of the important politicians are connected to various financial and industrial monopolies. Corruption is overt and lobbying ubiquitous. The changes are transforming Russia into a special kind of corporatist state, controlled by an influential oligarchy and with a high degree of criminal infiltration. The dangers of a shift toward authoritarianism are strong and may increase in the present political environment, unless there are strong countervailing forces. The power struggles between the political *nomenklatura* and the industrial-financial oligarchy have also weakened state power in the areas that were supposed to play a crucial role in designing and implementing the marketization process. These struggles, and the weakening of the state, were responsible for the chaotic start to market-building and the various problems encountered since. Elementary moral standards are ignored and illegal acts and even crimes are covered up. This has made the emergent Russian market "wilder" than its counterparts in other ex-socialist countries.

It is also essential for Russia to reform its federal relations. These form one of the most complex aspects of political transformation, with a close bearing on the prospects for the economic transition. The regions and republics of the Russian Federation differ strongly in their levels of social and economic development. Indeed the development gap in terms of fixed assets and volume of industrial output is of the order of tens or even hundreds. The highest average income per capita is 6 to 12 times the lowest. Most members need subsidies from the federal budget, while only a handful, like Moscow, are net donors.

Relations between the federal centre and the regions are not uniformly regulated. In some cases there are agreements on the division of powers, allowing members a greater or lesser degree of autonomy. Relations with Tatarstan and Bashkirtostan and a number of other republics resemble a confederation more closely than a federation. Without a well-conceived regional policy in Moscow and after the gross miscalculations by the government over the reforms, the regions seek to distance themselves from the centre and ignore many government decisions. Of course there are close connections between politics and the economy surrounding regional problems as well. On the one hand, there is a need for development and stronger general federal principles in regulating the economic and social processes of the whole country, but without of course re-establishing a unitary state. On the other hand, it is important to maximize the financial autonomy and self-government of Federation members. Ethnic tensions and the development of separatist tendencies can only be avoided by a rational combination of the two approaches.

It must obviously be a federal responsibility to protect national security, pursue foreign and external-economic policy, and maintain a single, federal market and system of law and order. Also required is a federal system of social guarantees for the public, to provide aid and support for economically weaker regions and formulate structural policy. Healthy federal relations must rest on an economically and politically warranted demarcation between federal, regional, and municipal ownership. The volume and structure of federal and regional ownership must correspond with the functions of the various levels of governance and with the privatization process. This assumes first of all a well-structured budgetary system, with an appropriate division of tax and other revenue between the centre on the one hand and the regions and municipalities on the other, so that the latter enjoy an appropriate level of autonomy. The equipment and funds for their economic and social activities need to be ensured by a rational system of sharing responsibilities. However, none of this must be allowed to impede federal functions and tasks.

The situation is similar in many ways in other CIS countries. The democratization of their political systems in the post-Soviet area has been impeded by their totalitarian past to a much greater extent than was the case with the CEE countries. The multi-tiered political system collapsed when the Soviet Union fell apart. Independence for the former Soviet republics meant that one political tier – the imperial centre – had been removed, which brought important domestic changes as well. The end of the party-state system "nationalized" and in many ways simplified the structure of political power and administration. However, an essentially authoritarian system of power has remained, even though formal institutions of democracy were established: a multi-party system, national presidential and parliamentary elections, and greater freedom of expression.

Executive power in the Central Asian states and in Kazakhstan, Belarus, and Moldova is held by groups drawn from the upper and middle layers of the *nomenklatura*. Most CIS countries are presidential republics. Some presidents have acquired the post for life or for a long term, through a referendum, and they have extensive powers, especially in Turkmenistan, Uzbekistan, Azerbaijan, and Kazakhstan.

Often the presidency was obtained by the former first secretary of the republic's communist party. The old state institutions have been retained, including the militia and state security, and they are in an even more bureaucratic and corrupt state than before. The legislature is weak and rudimentary, and subordinate to or manipulated by the executive. The media are controlled by the executive as well, or else by an industrial and financial oligarchy. These arrangements have made it easier to maintain law and order and regulate the course of market reforms. But they have also placed obstacles in their path, by hampering the emergence of new policies and a market mentality.

Parliamentary elections in most CIS countries follow a majority electoral system that allows the authorities to slow the development of a multi-party system and manipulate election campaigns. In some cases the authorities appear to have deliberately splintered the political spectrum, to prevent any party becoming a serious political alternative to the ruling regime or party in power. While the opposition parties in Russia have remained an influential political force, the political opposition is restricted and often persecuted in Central Asia, Kazakhstan, Azerbaijan, Georgia, and Belarus.

The heightened sense of national identity and delight at gaining state independence and sovereignty have helped to maintain political stability and led to some consolidation of society in the CIS countries. The fact that most of the public considers it will be easier to attain economic and social progress within the framework of one's own state has assured the top national political élite of a credit of trust. The strong presidential power in Uzbekistan, Turkmenistan, and Kazakhstan justifies itself by referring to the need to maintain political stability. On the other hand, no CIS country has yet managed to accomplish was what expected of independent national development. National independence has not proved a *sufficient* condition for supplying the needs of everyday life. It has not changed the grim economic realities. In several CIS countries, the national ideology is gradually losing its power to mobilize the public. It is increasingly understood that surmounting the deep economic crisis in which the CIS countries find themselves will mean looking beyond narrow nationalism, an ideology of kinship and clan, to the potentials of political democracy, to well-defined, socially oriented market reforms, and to equitable international cooperation. Nationalism alone may lead only to a protracted state of economic stagnation, a malfunctioning market, and internal instability that precipitates increasingly authoritarian forms of government.

An important issue related to democratization and market development is the role of the Russian state. Russia traditionally was strongly etatist even before the October Revolution. The problem is more acute still in less developed CIS countries. There the state organizations need to elaborate a structural policy and an incomes policy, as instruments of indicative planning and a reference point in corporate production strategy and budget and credit policy. Of course state support for scientific and technical progress, programmes for raising competitiveness in various industries and types of production, and definition of tariff and exchange-rate policies are important postulates in Western industrial countries as well.

There are diametrically opposite views about the role the state should play in the transition to a market economy. In Russia and some other CIS countries, opponents of shock therapy and monetarism accuse the government and state of being weak, of not using their authority, of being helpless in the fight against crime, and of failing to provide the institutional conditions for introducing an efficient market system. The main argument is that the Russian state is financially insolvent and weakened by corruption and crime. The Russian president, like the opposition, has called for law and order within the state, urging it to be healthier and stronger, and to exert greater control over economic processes.

Others accuse the Russian state of excessive intervention. Business people in various sectors, private entrepreneurs, and heads of enterprises and local authorities wax indignant about the way the state stifles production and business activity with taxes and bureaucratic interference, so abetting fraud and tax evasion. Both these views contain some truth.

The Russian state has used its power mainly to distribute state-owned assets, instead of helping to build up the market, establishing efficient institutions, creating a competitive atmosphere, and ensuring strict compliance with market rules. Instead of reforming the system of public finance, it extorts taxes from the public and enterprises to replenish the depleted state coffers. In short, where there is a need for effective change, the state displays weakness, and where there is no need for such change, it tries to show its power. Unless the state regulates the market economy and intervenes actively in its formation, to provide the requisite social orientation, Russia and the other CIS countries are bound to develop the kind of wild, robber-baron capitalism typical of Europe in the seventeenth and eighteenth centuries.

Market freedom, without a state presence, law and order, and self-restraint by society's members, leads to savagery and chaos, and a threat of degradation of the country. This conclusion is also drawn by realistic public figures and scholars in the West. Democracy and economic liberalism embody vices as well as virtues, dangers that should not be underestimated. A market economy with untrammelled, unlimited freedom may have destructive results, opening the way for manipulation of democracy and the market mechanism.

The Russian state's chronic insolvency also tends to make it dependent on the goodwill of the opulent West and of its own new economic élite. Meanwhile the administrative apparatus is increasingly invaded by corruption and deprived of respect and authority.

These developments limit the influence on society it needs to exert to accomplish marketization.

The results of the reforms in Russia and the other CIS countries depend largely on the extent to which the legislature lays the legal foundations for the functioning of the market, and the executive ensures that the law applies in practice.

Except in Russia, the reforms in the CIS countries have not strongly affected the role of the state in the economy. The inertia of the centralized command economy and the specific features of political development have meant that the state in most countries, notably Uzbekistan, Turkmenistan, Kazakhstan, and Belarus, has retained extensive scope for directing economic activity on the macro and micro levels. This partly explains why state expenditure forms so high a proportion of GDP in Tajikistan (54.5 per cent in 1994), Ukraine (45.0 per cent), Uzbekistan (33.0 per cent), and Belarus (33.0 per cent).

This leaves a serious dilemma for the future. For Russia to have a strong, influential state can be seen as a retreat into authoritarian, dictatorial rule, or alternatively, as progress toward a democratic, market-based system of law and order, with a democratic political culture, moral principles, and social responsibility. The development of such a state would require social accord on the main aims and methods of economic transformation, and consequently a search for compromise between the government and the opposition. An important change would also be required in the mass media. Regrettably, the ultimate goals of the reforms are either formulated too vaguely or passed over in silence. This produces an ideological vacuum that tends to paralyse people's creative energies. Hence, for instance, there is a feverish quest for a nationwide Russian idea that could rally and mobilize society.

In my view, the strategic objectives of transition should be seen in the context of the interrelation between politics and the economy. Neither the socialist planned economy nor the capitalist market economy have operated in harmony with their own ideals and theoretical models. Scientific and political rhetoric is one thing and real life another. Capitalism has undergone an evolution over the last century or so, to incorporate the postulates of new technology and social welfare. It has absorbed various elements that were previously associated with the concept and practice of socialism: social protection, forms of planning, the *de facto* role of the state, and democratization of property relations. So a transition in Russia to a wild, primitive type of capitalism would be counter-productive. The optimum would be a decentralized system, accepting various forms of ownership, including private ownership, development of market relations and institutions, and formation of a civil society and a lawful state. In effect this means the mixed economic system of the modern world, not a market transformation subject only to the laws of the jungle. It is necessary to strengthen state administration step by step, improving the selection and qualifications of officials, resolutely eradicating corruption, and reducing inflated staff to a reasonable size. In this connection, special attention should be paid to the armed forces, the judicial and penitentiary systems, and the presidential and governmental administrations.

A fresh start on reforms implies initiative and intervention on the part of the state with the object of creating a competitive environment in the country, because that is the core element of a market economy. As a result of ill-considered liberalization, state monopolies were replaced by private and criminal monopolies thirsting for easy gain. The state is faced with the task of ensuring effective control of natural monopolies and eliminating mafiosi groupings, which have established an illicit "cover" for many banks, for an overwhelming part of wholesale and retail trade, and many of the most profitable industries and enterprises.

A tax reform should be urgently undertaken with the aim of lowering taxation to a level that allows profitable production of goods and services at viable enterprises. This would make it unnecessary to resort to various dodges and fraud to evade taxes. Simultaneously, it is important to toughen administrative and criminal liability for tax evasion. Today, the risk of evasion is justified with the plea that ordinary enterprises would otherwise be unable to survive.

In contrast to the Western practice of privatization, which usually begins with loss-making enterprises, in Russia it was the most profitable enterprises that were primarily handed over into private ownership and sold off. As a result of such a suicidal policy, the state treasury became empty and the state itself was faced with the threat of bankruptcy. In order to avert it, the market was flooded with vast quantities of short-term (from a few weeks to a few months) government obligations with effective yields ranging from 30 per cent to 100 per cent. Accordingly, the Central Bank fixed high rates of refinance. This financial pyramid eventually came down, but its existence over a period of years siphoned off accumulations from the real sector of the economy to the speculative sector. The government and the Central Bank will inevitably have to abandon such practices and switch to the maintenance of a discount rate on credits acceptable to producers.

A revision of anti-inflationary policy is also on the agenda. The monetarist antidote has done little to cure the economy's woes. Due to a drastic reduction in the money supply, the economy has begun to suffer from a lack of money. The working capital of enterprises has shrunk below every conceivable limit. The ratio of the M2 money aggregate to the GDP has decreased from 79 per cent in 1990 to 13 per cent in 1998. In the industrially advanced countries of the West, and even in Eastern European countries in transition, this ratio is three to four times higher. The money supply shortfall, estimated at 300 trillion roubles (equal to the actual M2), is being substituted by surrogate "money," such as barter deals, foreign hard currencies, promissory notes, and mutual non-payments. These signify not only dislocations in the monetary system, but also considerable losses of the state budget, which has been deprived of emission income. The volume of US dollars circulating within the country (approximately US$ 40 billion in banknotes) is comparable to the volume of circulating roubles. This is not only forgone budgetary income, but also an inadmissible long-term and interest-free credit granted to the US and other Western countries.

Proposals have been voiced for the introduction, in parallel to the existing rouble, of a hard and freely convertible currency, the chervonets. Such an approach justified itself during the period of the New Economic Policy (NEP). The chervonets should be reliably backed with gold, foreign currency, and other liquid assets, and should give advantages in opening bank deposits and in domestic and external settlements. Regrettably, following all the failures, it is hard to expect the chervonets to command the required confidence, and without that it cannot win recognition on the market. However, such confidence could be produced through cooperation in the issue of the new currency between the central banking institutions of Russia and the European Union, with our orientation towards the Euro.

If the state is to put an end to the precipitous flight of capital from Russia (some US$ 100–150 billion in the years of the radical reforms), it cannot do without toughening up foreign-currency control and restrictions.

The role of morality and culture in marketization

A successful transition to a socially oriented market economy depends not only on the nature and direction of evolution of the political system, but on the general level of culture and morality in society.

Regrettably, analysts pay less than due attention to this key aspect of market transformation, which lies outside the sphere of pure economics or even politics, though it may be crucial to understanding the outcome of reforms. If political and economic changes towards democracy and the market are to attain their purpose, they must be accompanied by measures to raise society's cultural and moral standards.

According to Marxist doctrine, the category of "justice" lies exclusively in the sphere of morality, and has no place in economic science. So moral principles can be ignored in the economic policy of a Marxist state. However, a real-life economy does not develop exclusively according to purely economic laws. It is influenced by the legal and moral norms prevalent in society and by the policy of the state. It hardly needs saying that this applies not only in Russia and the CIS and CEE countries, but also in the West.

Market relations are regulated by legal norms, but the importance to the formation of a socially oriented market economy of having a healthy moral climate in society should not be underestimated. The law cannot be all-embracing. It has gaps that omit various aspects of economic activity or types of economic relations. These may be exploited by self-seekers, who make money at the expense of society as a whole. This is analogous to cases where the property of others is misappropriated, through burglary, robbery, fraud, and the like, which all agree in seeing as crimes.

The privatization of publicly owned assets using political power, connections, corrupt practices, and financial pyramids organized not only by private companies but by the finance ministry poses a challenge to moral concepts, while apparently remaining compatible with market relations. Covert, immoral, but not always illegal methods of getting rich include laundering money, using insider information on the stock exchange, and so on. Another way of covertly cheating others is to delay paying wages and pensions.

The confidence of business partners in each other and in the authorities setting the rules of the game is extremely important to healthy, civilized market relations. Any system displays legal loopholes or ambiguities. So a degree of mutual trust is required between partners, and there must also be safeguards against the state deceiving its citizens and foreign partners. Moral concepts like honesty and business reputation constitute buttresses of a modern market economy that are clearly being underestimated in Russia and the other CIS countries, where deception of partners or consumers has more or less become a rule. It is not surprising that the sad experiences of the past have produced in Russia a distrust of the country's monetary and financial institutions, avoidance of the national currency and preference for the US dollar. This is a sensitive factor behind the inflation and economic slump.

What is immoral in society's eyes cannot be economically effective, and cannot become a sound, solid element of a socially oriented market economy. Regrettably, the institutions of the Russian state do not square with this. They have done nothing to promote moral principles into public life and the economy. Moral criteria are likewise absent from the media's presentation of economic change. Nothing is done to cultivate modesty, condemn conspicuous consumption, promote decency and honesty, advance fellow-feeling and concern for others' interests, or respect the individual, regardless of social status. This moral hiatus is a sad additional problem during Russia's political and economic transition.

Note

1. It is over 10 years since the start of the Gorbachev reforms, and over 6 years since the 1989 revolutions in the CEE countries, which inaugurated a radical social transformation. There has been invaluable experience with reforms in this period, and except in former Yugoslavia, these have proceeded without serious social or military conflicts. The experience is instructive in many respects, including the interrelations between political and economic change. Comparisons of the market reforms taking place in the post-Soviet area also suggest some useful conclusions on this score. However, the process of transformation is far from complete, of course, so that some lessons from it are only of relative value.

5

Interactions between political and economic factors in the democratic transformation of Ukraine

Youri M. Matseiko

The relations between political transformation (particularly the democratization process) and economic transformation show some general characteristics and several *country-specific* attributes in all the former socialist countries. Dominance of the latter is an important feature of the changes in Ukraine, which is the second largest successor state to the Soviet Union. The transition to a democratic market economy is affected by the country's ethnic diversity, its religious division, its inherited level of economic development, and its structural deficiencies. Another important specific factor is that the transition coincides with the building of a political and economic infrastructure for independent statehood. Although the country had several national institutions while it was a member of the Soviet Union, these had limited powers and responsibilities.

All these factors are complicating the changes and making them slower and harder than initially expected. Progress toward a new model for a democratic market economy, based on respect for human rights and on economic prosperity, has been modest and faulting. Ukraine at the end of the 1990s remains in deep political, economic, and social crisis. This background makes the interactions between democratization and economic reforms complex, controversial, and problematic.

The state of the economic transformation

After independence was gained, there was strong revulsion against the practices of a centrally planned economy, especially because of its inefficiency and shortcomings under the Soviet Union. Concurrently there was a strong attraction towards an often idealized perception of a market system. The achievements of Western countries were overestimated, while the shortcomings of market economies and the socio-economic requirements for sustaining a developed market system were almost ignored. So there was a widespread erroneous belief that transforming Ukraine into a market economy was not going to be difficult; with independent statehood, it would bring a rapid, substantial rise in the standard of living. Events proved otherwise, and the consequent disillusionment has contributed to a curious reform fatigue and political apathy in the country. The transition process has become slow, unstable, and marginal.

Of course there has been some progress with creating democratic institutions and transforming the centrally planned economy into a market system, but the economic and social costs have been higher than expected. Two particularly painful aspects have been the drastic, more or less unbroken fall in output and the rise in unemployment. Some problems were to be expected in the transition period, but the decline has been exceptionally deep, long, and wide-ranging in Ukraine. The fall in GDP between 1990 and 1996 was 61.6 per cent – GDP in 1997 was 35.4 per cent of what the GDP had been in 1990. In 1996 the contraction was 10.1 per cent and in 1997 it was 3.0 per cent.[1] There are no reliable statistics for unemployment, which is one of the most serious problems of the transition process. The obvious reason for this is that many of the unemployed omit to register officially. They simply do not believe they will get outside help. There are many citizens who are officially at work, but produce nothing and receive no remuneration. The unpaid wage, pension, and stipend bills are enormous and increased in volume nine times between January 1996 and June 1997.[2] The government has no programme, plan, or timetable, and many private firms fail to take resolute, urgent measures to remunerate people. There are vague promises by the government, but nothing actually changes.

This serious social failure could lead to a dangerous, explosive situation with unpredictable consequences. The social-security system is in a parlous state. The old system has been dismantled, but a new one has yet to be created. The state simply manifests its incompetence

95

and impotence in the face of the situation, and so does the private sector. So Ukraine suffers a rapid decline in social protection. Meanwhile the inequality of income distribution steadily increases. The problems are compounded by widespread corruption and organized crime, which impede the development of a real market economy and pose a serious threat to democracy. For corrupt groups do not simply lack an interest in developing democracy, they prefer authoritarianism. The transformational recession in Ukraine has developed into a veritable crisis. The drastic contrast between expectations and outcome is one source of the deep political and social tensions in the country.[3]

The situation in Ukrainian agriculture deteriorated particularly fast. An effective agricultural policy would require a radical refurbishment of economic, social, and legal relations. The measures for restructuring land ownership and redistributing the means of production, to increase output, are developing quite slowly. There are serious management problems with the new structures, such as joint-stock companies and other corporate units in agriculture. The cooperatives are still run by their former managers and communist-party functionaries. It is crucial, in a country where the rural population remains important and the security of food supplies is a vital issue, to effect a far-reaching reform of the agricultural sector. This is also indispensable to the success of democratization.

Ukrainian industry finds itself in a vicious circle. Privatization is slow. Without a substantial increase in operating capital, enterprises have been unable to break out of the recession. The state has no money to do this. The only real possibility that remains is to attract foreign direct investment, but investors have been in no hurry to go into Ukraine, because the general investment climate is unfavourable. In any case, all possible ways of facilitating access to foreign capital must be explored, and confidence in the country's political future strengthened. Free movement of foreign capital must be insured. That is the crux of the matter, the only way to attain a rise in national production and boost business activity, which will ultimately contribute to democratizing the economy and politics as well.

An assessment made recently by the Harvard Institute for International Development correctly states that:

high subsidies, along with slow privatization, slow deregulation and high taxes, have disabled economic growth. A peculiar vicious circle has emerged in which, due to slow reforms, a declining economy generates less and less real income and results in further sluggishness of reforms, which leads to a further decrease of incomes, and so on.[4]

The two basic premises for consolidating the economy – financial stability and liberal market framework – require major reforms and increasing efficiency in governance.

A fundamentally important dimension of the prolonged economic and social crisis in Ukraine is in essence a *crisis of state power*. Successful creation of a modern, effective market economy must include reform of state functions, which entails restoring and reinforcing the authority of the state. This means first of all that citizens and economic actors must respect the laws of the state. There has been no shortage of various government strategies and programmes, which rightly identify such tasks as stabilization, liberalization, creation of market institutions, and privatization. However, there have been no practical linkages made between these tasks, which have been related even less to democratization or redefining the role of the state.[5]

It must be added that the reforms in Ukraine were effectively stalled until the end of 1994. President Kuchma indicated that by then the state of the Ukrainian economy had reached a point where the efforts made to lift administrative controls had led to a weakening of the state's influence on the real economic processes.[6] The tax base and the system of currency regulation had been undermined. All this, along with the strong Soviet traditions, actually amounted to a *continuation* of the centralization policies. As a result local authorities were ignoring the centre's decisions, which was bad for the Ukrainian economy and bad for Ukrainian democracy. Since 1994, the process of market transformation has begun, but rather slowly and unevenly and with a number of shortcomings. For example, the lack of interaction between liberalization, stability, privatization, and structural reform is essentially artificial and destructive.

Liberalization would normally imply first the abandonment of many economic functions and controls practised by the state under the centrally planned system. In Ukraine, however, the pretext of strengthening the state's economic management had constrained the liberalization process, while the necessary functions of the state were being undermined, particularly in the social sphere. The outcome was chaos in the economy.

Stabilization policies have been proclaimed many times, but the results have been limited and counter-productive. As mentioned already, the decline in production continues. Inflation has slowed, but it has not been contained. Demonetization, which cannot be equated with stabilization, is proceeding fast. At the beginning of 1995, the money supply was equal to 63 per cent of GDP. At the end of 1995 it was 20 per cent, and in 1996 only 9 per cent.[7] Inflation and the budget deficit are being curbed at the expense of high unemployment and poverty. Many people are desperately trying to survive by all possible means (unregistered incomes, petty trading in foreign goods, dwarf agricultural holdings, etc.) Such a desperate state of affairs cannot be considered a real stabilization.

The first privatization act was adopted in 1993, but nothing substantial was achieved in the first few years. The process has accelerated since 1995, following lines similar to those in Russia and some other former socialist countries. The managers of former state-owned enterprises (SOEs) have simply taken on new functions, as presidents or chief executives of newly created companies and groups. In spite of the slogans and promises to transfer assets to broad masses of the population, this has not taken place. The so-called privatization certificates distributed are actually senseless and useless, and ignored by the private sector. Privatization has brought little improvement in the performance of firms. Ten per cent have managed to increase their capital value and improve their business. Another 10 per cent have improved their production potential by bringing in outside investors. That leaves 80 per cent of the SOEs in a poor situation, having been deprived of state subsidies and privileges.

All this has had serious political consequences, for the future of the economy and also for the development of democracy. There is hardly any sign of a middle class developing. Public views on the reform process tend to be negative. In a survey of public opinion, by the National Educational Programme for Market Transformation and the US Agency for International Development, 95 per cent of respondents rated Ukraine's economic situation as very bad or fairly bad, and only 4 per cent as good. Ukraine was thought by 49 per cent to be going the wrong way and by 33 per cent to be going the right way. The situation in the state had worsened according to 67 per cent and was unchanged according to 25 per cent.[8] The respondents saw as the underlying causes of the existing difficulties corruption (35 per cent), disruption of essential economic ties (23 per cent), poor work by officials (13 per cent), transition to a different economic system (13 per cent), the tax system (6 per cent). The government's actions were described as indecisive by 82 per cent and disordered by 71 per cent, while 81 per cent of the respondents put little or no trust in the government.[9] These opinions indicate that most people would support major changes to improve governance, eliminate bureaucratic arbitrary methods, decentralize political power, and create a public administration of qualified, honest, professional civil servants, committed to Ukrainian sovereignty and independence.

Democratization and socio-economic change

The process of creating a modern, democratic, pluralistic political system in Ukraine is at an early stage, with many tasks still to be accomplished. The biggest problem I see is the increasing public alienation from the political process. Passivity towards public life and widespread withdrawal from civil participation give strong cause for concern. Ordinary people are taken up with their struggle to survive and find an adequate means of making a living. This makes the political process in Ukraine somewhat unusual. Political activity is becoming livelier, but it has little to do with the broad masses. It concerns only an upper echelon of politicians, business people, and criminal elements. So political life is becoming dirtier.

There is convincing evidence of this in the drastic decline in election turn-outs. The legislature (*Verkhovna Rada*) was operating in 1997 with about 50 seats vacant, after several elections and by-elections had failed to produce results. The same applies in many local assemblies. There is growing popular animosity against politicians, parliamentarians, and local deputies. One explanation lies in the economic difficulties experienced by many Ukrainians, for which they blame the political parties and their leaders.

Another source of distrust is the egotistical behaviour of many politicians. This raises a crucial question. What will be the consequences of such public alienation and dissatisfaction for the future course of democratic reforms in Ukraine? Is there a real danger of a backlash against democracy that might result in a form of totalitarian regime? This might take the form of an attempt by the ruling circles to safeguard their position under the pretext of averting chaos and restoring order. Regrettably, there are already developments that support such gloomy predictions.

Some of the problems derive from the weak institutional and political guarantees for the democratization process. The other source relates to the economic and social difficulties discussed already. As for institutional guarantees, a new democratic constitution was adopted in 1996. However, not even the most progressive best-written constitution can alone guarantee the political process, ethnic peace, or economic prosperity, because there are no constitutional remedies for destructive feelings of hatred and intolerance and other social tensions. The implementation of the constitution's provisions would require various institutional changes and reforms relating to democratization and economic transformation. As to the political side, both democracy and constitutional guarantees for human rights and liberties must have high priority. There must also be legal guarantees for ownership. Ownership reforms demand a stable lawful basis and firm guarantees. Property rights must be defended by law and respected accordingly. This is especially important in view of the strong populist feelings in the society. Many Ukrainians find egalitarian populist ideology attractive, and also hold the view that an expansion of private ownership increases income inequalities. The left-wing parties, especially the communists, try to take advantage of these feelings in every way they can. Unfortunately the government does not seem active enough in dealing with these dangerous developments.

The legal system needs to define more clearly the distribution of authority and responsibilities between the legislature, the executive, and the judiciary. The constitution does not state exactly who represents the executive, the president, or the government. There are strong tendencies in the presidency, the government, and the legislature to assume more power at the expense of others. Also in need of a strict, clear division of competence and rights is local government, especially in the context of property and finance. Two recent acts passed by the legislature cover local self-government and local self-government administration,[10] but there are still substantial problems with local finances and local property.

The power struggles within and between the three branches of power are more or less inevitable, but they are often caused by legal deficiencies. The problem has become increasingly an object of political pressure, and more importantly still, affects the various fields of reform.

State power in Ukraine means above all the power of the president. It is still unclear whether the president is head of the executive. If he is, what functions can the prime minister perform? The president's functions as defined in the constitution are somewhat vague: "safeguarding state independence, national security and the right of the state's succession."[11] There are also major problems with the cabinet of ministers. One is its buffer role. The tasks assigned to it by the president and the legislature sometimes contradict each other. The constitution stipulates that the cabinet prepare and implement state programmes of economic, social, and cultural development,[12] but does not state that these have to be adopted by the legislature and given the status of the statutory law. The legislature interferes in the day-to-day activities of the cabinet, playing an important role in the political process and in economic transformation. The constitution pays heed to the division of political powers, but the same is not the case with economic life. There special tensions exist and no interactions take place between the branches of power. This gap is being filled by clans, political and economic groups, regional formations, and so on.

The high turnover among political leaders, especially in the cabinet, coincides with a rapid succession of key civil servants and instability within the government accompanied by a lack of a clear policy orientation. These in many respects reflect also the weakness of all democratic institutions, the low political culture, and the poor capabilities for managing socio-political conflicts by democratic means. Ukraine simply does not know what constructive political opposition means. This all goes some way to explaining why it is almost impossible to reach the kind of consensus among various political players that would make government feasible or viable.

During the early years of Ukraine's independence there was some kind of political consensus around rejecting the "socialist era," but even this fragile understanding was soon over, to be replaced by a deep contradiction between optimistic expectations and gloomy existing realities. Many express disappointment with the market economy, but that does not necessarily mean they wish the return to "real socialism." Nevertheless, they are far from happy with the results so far in economic, political, and social transformation.

Building the institutions for a sustainable democracy

Recognizing the strong interactions between political and economic processes and the weight of socio-economic difficulties does not mean that the principle of economic determinism has to be accepted. It would be equally wrong to deny the interdependence between the economic situation and the existing political regime,[13] and claim that in spite of a deep crisis in the economic and social spheres, Ukraine has become a democratic country in a European sense.

One of the crucial problems in every democratic system is to determine the extent to which people are duly protected by the law. From this point of view, democracy in Ukraine has to be viewed less as a static phase than as a dynamic process. A decisive stage was reached with the adoption of the new constitution. This enshrines such basic principles as the priority for human rights and freedoms, legal equality of citizens, democratic election of government, the division of powers, guarantees of human rights and freedoms, and the right to political opposition. This document certainly strengthens democracy in Ukraine. But to the question of whether totalitarianism is unthinkable or impossible, the answer is not easy. There is a democratic evolution of the political regime taking place, but this does not mean there is yet a strong and sustainable democracy. The system has elements of both democracy and totalitarianism, which interact and often counteract in different ways.

The dissolution of the Soviet Union, a stronghold of totalitarianism, has influenced Ukraine's democratic process in a positive way. Democracy has received a strong stimulus to develop further, but there remain some strong remnants of totalitarianism, which it would be unrealistic to ignore.[14]

In this sense one should not underestimate the existing human-rights violations in Ukraine, especially socio-economic rights: non-payment of wages and pensions, and the failure by the government to support health care, social security, science, culture, art, etc. All these evidently conflict with the provisions of the International Covenant on Economic, Social and Cultural Rights. These in particular are Articles 7 (the right to fair wages and equal remuneration for work of equal value, the right to a decent living), 11 (the right of everyone to an adequate standard of living, including adequate food, clothing, and housing, and to continuous improvement of living conditions) and 12 (the right of everyone to enjoyment of the highest attainable standard of physical and mental health).[15] So constant worsening of the socio-economic situation in the country is in itself a contradiction of human rights. There are violations of political rights as well, including the irresponsibility of bureaucrats who retain and strengthen their power in their own selfish interests and ignore the interests of the public. This is precisely where the real danger of totalitarianism lies in Ukraine. Functionaries are becoming independent of the law. They ignore it by introducing countless instructions, addenda, clarifications etc., until the law ultimately becomes powerless and meaningless.

The most powerful stronghold of totalitarianism in the former Soviet Union was the communist party. This was dissolved, but new communist parties have arisen. Communist functionaries have retained and indeed strengthened their hegemony in important branches of power and the economy. This ties in with the tendency to strengthen the ubiquitous regulatory activity of the state in economic life, which in this form marks a blow to the market transition.

Remembering all these considerations, the market economy cannot be seen as a guarantee of democracy. It may contribute to it, but for it to do so requires the existence of a middle class, whose absence is one of the weakest points of the democratic process in Ukraine. What has been occurring, in fact, is the opposite of embourgeoisement: mass speedy impoverishment of the whole population, and emergence of a tiny handful of very rich. There are growing divisions and atomization of Ukrainian society, bringing serious dissatisfaction, contradictions, and potential for conflict. Under these circumstances, the power of the state may turn increasingly towards violent methods, which amounts to taking the dangerous path towards totalitarianism.

However, political parties and organizations are beginning to play an important role in democratization. There were more than 40 in existence in mid-1997. Practically all parties are relatively small: the Communists have 140,000 members, the Liberals 55,000, the People's Rukh 55,000, the Socialists 34,000, and Labour 31,000.[16] Of course, Ukraine is not alone in this. There are many non-mass political parties in the world. Extremely important here are such factors as programmes, strategy, tactics, and methods of influencing the electorate. These are what political parties in Ukraine lack. What they need most of all is a body of new economic, political, and social ideas, and talented and honest leaders. The experiences of the parliamentary elections of 1998 indicated that the large number of parties and elections in itself did not result in a well-functioning, pluralistic, multi-party system. Many parties have been formed just for the sake of elections. The presidential circles preparing for the elections have been trying for example to create a "party of power." A special role has been designated for the People's Democratic Party and for the "New Ukraine" movement. In December 1996, a permanent consultative council of certain political parties (the People's Democrats, the Agrarian, Democratic Liberal and Labour parties, Rukh, etc.) was established.[17] Something similar has been organized under the auspices of the speaker of the legislature, with the Communists and the Socialists as the main participants. These left-wing parties have been actively exploiting the critical, tense situation in society, and this shows a desperate longing for state power. There are nine party factions in the *Verkhovna Rada*, the Unkrainian parliament. The most influential are Communists (115), People's Rukh (42), Gromada (40), People's Democrats (27), etc. Strangely enough there is no ruling party which forms the cabinet. The president and the prime-minister in fact represent no political party. That means in fact non-party state power in the country. This phenomenon is a vivid example of the functioning of civil society as well. The parties do practically nothing to overcome political passivity in the people. They do not actually feel any responsibility for the economic, financial, and social crisis.

Ukraine has yet to develop a pluralistic, multi-party, democratic self-governing infrastructure, including a civilized opposition. The opposition forces that exist are extremely diverse, and given to fighting each other in a non-constructive way. In reality the sharp quarrels may be seen as skirmishes between clans over privatization portions. This so-called opposition is weak in the sense that it lacks serious, constructive strategies, programmes, and so on that correspond to the wishes of the people.

Ukraine is still in search of an electoral system, a vital aspect of the political process. In principle there are two options, first-past-the-post and proportional representation, with many combined systems in between them. The electoral law adopted in September 1997 is such a combined system. Through the former element, the very wealthy and powerful can gain a special advantage. Such factors are present in any election. In Ukraine, the roles of official-bureaucrat or manager-employer are endowed with special influence. It is usual for officials from the executive branch to enter the legislature, which is dangerous, because it means those in power give themselves their orders and ordinary people become alienated from the authorities. There is no trace in Ukraine of a Hatch Act, the 1939 measure in the United States outlawing participation in legislative power and work in electoral districts by administration officials. Functionaries and managers control elections in several ways, and the scope for them to do so is increased by the first-past-the-post element in the electoral system.

Proportional representation gives a better reflection of the electors' opinions. It makes electoral districts more justifiable and gives greater chances of influencing the deputy elected. There are also arguments against this option. One is that it produces a legislature containing several parties, none of them massive or influential enough to provide a strong government. Some problems of this kind certainly exist in Ukraine, but this cannot and should not prevent the political process being strengthened through the activity of various parties. The main aspect of the problem is that it is being actively discussed within the highest political ranks – parliamentarians, government officials and members of the president's staff. Only one very important factor is absent, and that is the voice of the people, who on this as on many other subjects remain silent.

Only sporadic public opinion polls reveal the views of the public on certain important issues, such as the reforms in the country. In January of 1998 for example this question was asked in the framework of a special national poll: is it worthwhile to continue reforms in Ukraine? Forty-six per cent was in favour, 24 per cent against, 36 per cent could not give a definitive answer. The proportion of "radical supporters of reforms" declined between 1994 and 1997 from 29.6 per cent to 20.3 per cent and the number of "conservatives" increased from 30.9 per cent to 38 per cent.

Having lived through a series of economic shocks during the first years of *perestroika* people are not expecting any more miracles from the market. The majority of the population is, however, not against development of the market economy. Positive attitudes to private enterprise still remain fairly strong. The crucial questions which are being asked are in whose interests these transformations are taking place. Is the level of well-being of the masses increasing or declining? Are we creating a wild capitalism with the law of the jungle or a socially oriented market economy?

Reforms in Ukraine have not yet become irreversible. Success in business depends (as was the case in the past) on availability of state resources which are distributed by influential functionaries. Ukraine still stands at the threshold of an extremely important choice: moving toward a quasi-democratic state with corporate, criminal influences or developing on a path of building a normal, Western-type democratic market economy. While the restoration of communist power is unlikely, at the same time one cannot exclude possible political shocks, further increases in corruption and lawlessness in a combination of democracy and oligarchy.

Another extremely important issue shaping the political process in Ukraine is the interconnections and interactions between the political and economic élites. Those who own property often perform political functions directly, while former members of the *nomenklatura* and other high social groups often use their power to obtain property. With the new owners of wealth active in politics, there is a serious danger to democracy from corruption in high places and from organized crime. These two phenomena coexist and also interact. They have no use for democracy, which they see as harmful to their interests and try to obstruct in every way. The government, unfortunately, acts ineptly and inefficiently to prevent this. No major steps to fight corruption and organized crime have been taken. A few programmes for doing so have been announced and some new governmental structures have been created, but nothing has been done to examine the substance of the problem and its underlying roots and causes. This dangerous situation in Ukraine is viewed with anxiety in many other countries.

In this context, several useful recommendations for Ukraine may be found in the proceedings of the European Conference of Ministers of Justice, organized by the Council of Europe in June 1997. Attention was drawn to the danger of interaction between corruption and organized crime. The conference stated that corruption was undermining the basis of democracy in Eastern and Western Europe. Another very dangerous development is the internationalization of corruption. This makes united international action an urgent task. An international legal basis has to be created. The European Union has set up an international group on corruption to prepare a programme called "Octopus," and Ukraine is participating in this. There are two international conventions (criminal and civil) being prepared, and the European Union is also working on a code of conduct for state officials.[18]

Of the factors that exert a positive influence on democratic processes in Ukraine, there is the stable, generally calm situation concerning the various national and ethnic minorities. The specific geopolitical situation of the country, with its East-West divide, gives added importance to questions of multi-ethnic development. There are objective assimilation processes taking place, but at the same time there exists freedom to preserve national identity. This naturally includes the Russian community, which for important reasons cannot be considered as a national minority. The Russians hold a special role and place in Ukraine's national situation. There is no discrimination whatsoever against them, or against other national groups in Ukraine. Relations are free of suspicion and distrust and based on friendship and cooperation.

The policies Ukraine pursues on ethnic issues bring it closer to possessing a real civil society. (The same cannot always be said of other CIS countries.) The new constitution states clearly that the Ukrainian people are an aggregate of Ukrainian citizens belonging to all nationalities. That brings the country to an important understanding of a nation as one of co-citizenship. Of course there is a need to imbue this understanding with real social substance, which will take time and hard work. However, Ukraine can already claim to have freed itself to a large extent from a narrow ethnic outlook, and it exists as a multinational country without inter-ethnic conflicts. The prominent public-opinion and market-research organization Socis-Gallup clearly concluded that the explanation for this positive phenomenon lies in self-awareness, in the mentality of the Ukrainian people, whose way of life is marked by a strong culture of contacts, goodwill, and toleration between ethnic groups.[19]

There are also some unfavourable tendencies. Some left-wing parties want to restore the notion of a "unified Soviet people." Such deceptive ideas cause a reaction in various radical forces, which stand for a "national revolution." Both approaches are dangerous, and may raise obstacles to attaining a truly democratic society in Ukraine.

The vast majority of people stand for a simple and just approach: let Ukraine be the common home of all who live in its territory. In the Socis-Gallup survey, 80 per cent of respondents agreed with that statement. National diversity is a real asset. The idea of sustaining cultural diversity is not at odds with the fact that the Ukrainian people pay special attention to traditional spiritual and cultural values, and support nationhood, including the use and purity of the Ukrainian language and development of Ukrainian culture. Furthermore, these are considered as priorities by the state. This can also be seen as a natural reaction to a long and hard history of "denationalization" policies.

Some conclusions

Ukraine is going through a hard, rather long period of transition that opens up many new opportunities, but brings some unprecedented problems. Some of these problems are familiar to many parts of the world. Others are specific to Ukraine. Politicians and economists in the country are tending to view the market economy, social policy, and the process of democratization as three distinct areas. There is insufficient understanding that an integrated approach demands simultaneous, not sequential progress towards the goals of production growth, social justice, and real democracy. It is not right to stress all the time the absolute priority of the economy. Ukraine has to give priority to economic policies that not only contribute to increasing output, but promote social equity and democracy as well. It is not enough to note the redistributive impact of social policy. Its effects on productivity and democratization must also be considered. There are problems in Ukraine with creating the socio-economic framework for sustainable democracy. What is good for the market economy may not be good for democracy, and vice versa. Instead of a decentralization of economic power, it is common in Ukraine to see a concentration of it, in the form of various kinds of monopoly. This favours authoritarianism rather than democracy.

There is a widening gap between rich and poor. Mass poverty, unemployment, and extreme differences of wealth are increasing. With these unfavourable processes in mind, it has to be concluded that there is no solid basis for political or economic democratization in Ukraine. The system of social security has glaring deficiencies.

The Ukrainian political system does not fit either of the traditional schemes of democracy or authoritarianism. It should not be forgotten that Ukraine suffers a great burden from its Soviet past. However, it has managed to acquire some promising qualities, of which the new democratic constitution is a vivid example. On the other hand, this positive document has yet to be applied constructively. So the Ukrainian position can be said to be one in which there is a constant, fairly tense struggle between democracy and authoritarianism. The specific of this process is confrontation within the power structure itself. This takes the form of a struggle for access to the main instruments of power and for control over property, waged by various financial and venture-capital groups that have already consolidated, by the agrarian lobby, by the military industrial complex, by regional clans, and so on. The gap between them and the people is growing dangerously wide.

One of the weakest points in Ukrainian democracy today is the absence of mass active participation in the political process. This situation is being exploited by strong authoritarian forces. Ordinary people do not seem interested in participating in national politics. The main reason is probably the dire economic and social situation in the country, where people simply strive to exist by all possible ways and means, preoccupied with the immediate problem of non-payment of wages, pensions, and social benefits. This surrenders the political arena to various clans, élites, political parties (or rather political clubs), and regional and other groups. The broad masses seem silent, passive, and indifferent, and simply not interested in organizing themselves, even to protect their crucial rights. All these uncertainties and weaknesses complicate the political process in Ukraine, make the task of institutionalization in economic and social life more difficult. At the same time, they activate various directions, approaches, and ways to escape from dangerous developments. In some ways this helps society to adjust and survive. The apathy and fragmentation of Ukrainian society are becoming (strange though may it sound) an important driving force for stability. The Ukrainian people – not forgetting the tough lessons of their long and dramatic history – are learning to rely on themselves and move ahead towards a stable future.

Notes

1. *Zerkalo Nedely*, 19 April 1997.
2. *Uriadovy Kurier*, 3 July 1997.
3. Describing the state of Ukraine's economy, President L. Kuchma emphasized in a report on Constitution Day, 27 June 1997 that "stabilization of the economic situation has not been achieved – one may speak only of a slowing in the tempo of the crisis processes. Moreover, after adoption of the Constitution, we have not only failed to achieve a substantial acceleration of the economic reforms, we have put a visible brake on them ... The situation is not being improved, basically because the recession in production and the imbalance of the budget system are not being overcome. The payments crisis is becoming especially acute."
4. *Opinion*, 31 July–6 August 1997.
5. Hesse, J.J., ed. (1995), *Administrative Transformation in Central and Eastern Europe. Towards Public Sector Reform in Post-communist Societies*, Cambridge, Mass.: Harvard Institute for Economic Development, p. 78.
6. *Uriadovy Kurier*, 27 October 1994.
7. *Golos Ukrainy*, 21 January 1994.
8. *Pidtext*, 21–27 May 1997.
9. Ibid.
10. *Golos Ukrainy*, 12 June 1997.
11. *Constitutzia Ukrainy*, 1997.
12. Ibid.
13. Hesse (1995), p. 126.
14. *Pidtext*, 23 April–6 May 1997.
15. "International Covenant on Economic, Social and Cultural Rights," in UN (1973), *Human Rights. A Compilation of International Instruments of the United Nations*, New York: United Nations, pp. 3–5.
16. *Zerkalo Nedely*, 17 April 1997.
17. *Pidtext*, 7–20 May 1997, 9–15 September 1998, 28 October–3 November 1998.
18. *Izvestiya*, 11 June 1997.
19. *Izvestiya*, 11 October 1997.

6

The politics of privatization in Croatia: Transition in times of war

Ivan Grdešić

Last time I went by a certain wall in Ljubljana the graffiti were still there: "Let this democracy pass, so that we can live like human beings." That says a lot about the last seven years of transition, and not just in Slovenia. It summarizes plenty of "transitology" – an emerging sub-field of political science and political economy. It is a reminder of communist political culture, of politics operating in waves, in ideological campaigns that were always producing new content for party meetings, seeking to mobilize activists, and attempting to give some sort of substance to political life. In each case, citizens knew it would only be a short-lived campaign, soon giving way to something else that might well be its complete opposite. Is democracy just another political campaign? Will it give way to something else? These graffiti clearly try to convey three things: (i) political pluralism and the processes of multi-party democracy produce disturbance and flux; (ii) they engender social insecurity and economic hardship that contribute to a permanent loss of stability and security in everyday life; (iii) problems in the democratization process can provide fertile ground for a slowdown, or even a reversal of the transition process.

Croatia was early to join the Central and Eastern European (CEE) countries in their historic leap through the double doors of democracy and market. The doors seemed to point the way to Europe, towards democratic freedom and a Western standard of living. The political side of the transition began in the spring of 1990, with the first multi-party elections. Many other sides of this social transformation were soon to emerge, some quite unexpected and tragic. Croatia faced, apart from democratization and economic transition, the massive challenges of building a nation-state, after the socialist Yugoslav federation disintegrated, and of defending itself against domestic insurgence and outside aggression. The country faced several problems at once, any one of which would have sufficed as the life's work of a generation. Without a doubt, all its transition policies, political, social, and economic, have been profoundly influenced by the war and its aftermath.

Croatia's transition agenda covers more than a simple process of democratization. I will try in this paper to highlight some of these agenda items, with special emphasis on the privatization process. My working hypothesis is that the war dominated not only the political issues but the main aspects of privatization policy. The effort to defend the country from aggression (particularly after 1991) limited and directed institutional choices and policy options. Developing and defending the state became the ultimate criterion in national decision-making. Only in an independent state could democracy and capitalism be realized. These priorities were shaped and configured "internally" by the dominant political ideology of the new ruling party, the political concepts of its leaders, and the social and cultural values.[1]

The transition agenda

The post-communist agenda in all CEE countries is crowded with redistributive items.[2] Redistributive policies involve a high level of conflict, large parts of the population (often the entire population), big changes in the distribution of social resources and power, and long time-frames. The radical policies that were announced by the new government after the electoral defeat of the communists indeed concerned large numbers of people and major social groups and an inherently high conflict potential. They included denationalization and privatization, integration of Croats abroad into the homeland, redefinition of Croatia's position within the Yugoslav Federation, spiritual renewal and a return to cultural traditions, a new state administration, and changes in the national structure of state agencies (the police and army). At the same time, there were identification decisions concerning the state, its citizens, and the political, economic, and social system. The decisions on these redistributive issues had to be taken quickly, in most cases during the new governing party's first term of office. The only indisputable asset the new government had was electoral victory, which was generally seen as conferring legitimacy on the transition in Croatia.

While these were the tasks the new political authorities aspired to undertake, the social and economic environment did not change much in the first couple of years. Although the political hegemony of the communists had ceased, many elements of the period remained: the economic system, social structure and political culture, the weakness of civil society, the apparatus of state, and even the communists themselves.[3] The political scene was additionally burdened with the processes of disintegration of the Yugoslav Federation, and the first indications of armed Serbian opposition to the new government. This developed in less than a year into fully fledged aggression and war on land, in the air, and at sea. There was also a state of flux internationally. Western governments and the various international agencies, baffled by the magnitude, speed, and quality of the changes in the region, failed to respond to the rapidly developing crisis in the Yugoslav region. There was no political initiative or appropriate military resources forthcoming to prevent or contain the escalation of the war in Croatia, and later Bosnia-Herzegovina.

Croatia's new political élite realized the extent of the tasks ahead, which the president-elect, Dr. Franjo Tudjman, listed in his first address to the nation, after the first, founding elections in 1990. Tudjman announced a 10-point strategic programme that set the redistributive national agenda for the following decade and beyond. It produced new actors, people, and groups to implement that agenda, so that it constituted a mobilization of all state and social resources to apply the new concepts over a lengthy period of time. It also heralded major changes for all Croatian citizens, on a local and personal, as well as a national level.

The 10 "immediate tasks" were these:[4]

1. The new Constitution of the Republic of Croatia must be free of ideological content, based on Croatian state-building laws, and compiled in line with the most advanced democratic traditions of contemporary European and North American reality and jurisprudence.

2. Regarding the new constitutional position of Croatia within Yugoslavia, Croatian sovereignty must be ensured on a confederate basis, through a contractual confederation of sovereign states.
3. Croatia must join Europe and become Europeanized. Croatia must gain its identity and accelerate its development through European integration.
4. A state of law must be established and the state administration modernized. There must be separation of the legislative, executive, and judiciary branches. The judiciary must be free from political influence and completely independent.
5. There must be a spiritual renewal that creates the conditions for eliminating all harmful divisions among the Croatian people.
6. Radical changes are required in property and economic relations. There is a need for denationalization and re-privatization.
7. Demographic revival must be ensured by preventing emigration and increasing the birth rate.
8. Returning emigrés must be reintegrated into society.
9. There is a need for change in the public services. This requires urgent and major changes in almost all areas of public life (culture, science, education, health care, newspapers, etc.)
10. There must be moral renewal and a revival of the work ethic. Traditional values and moral norms corrupted and debased by existing socialism must be restored, primarily through the family and the school.

Although privatization comes sixth on the list, below the state-building objectives, it features in a very clear and open way. As I mentioned, privatization was to be used to further some other items on this list that do not belong directly to the economic sphere.

Social values, institutional choices, and political activities

Croatia started privatizing in April 1991. (More precisely, it had started on that path with the policy of economic stabilization and restructuring put forward in July 1990 by the then prime minister of the Socialist Federal Republic of Yugoslavia, Ante Marković.) This was a month before Croatia's referendum on independence and only a year after the first democratic elections. While the clouds of conflict were already visible on the federal horizon, the big venture ahead was encouraged by the "old-new" social values being advanced. The values predominantly chosen by citizens at the beginning of 1990 were political: peace, European integration, national identity, and social justice. Private entrepreneurship was a value choice of only 5 per cent of respondents in a representative poll taken at this time.[5] Nevertheless, people were ready to take responsibilities in the economic sector and they wanted only a moderate level of state intervention in the economy. Altogether 48 per cent wanted to terminate the system of socialist self-management, the notable (infamous) invention of the Yugoslav communist regime, and give full authority to company management. Of the respondents engaged in private, mainly small-scale business, 83 per cent called for full independence from state control. These data indicate the positive climate of opinion for future privatization decisions, and the general acceptance of the need to abandon and alter the socialist political and economic system.

However, one set of data stood out as a warning that the new political élite, soon also to be the economic élite, would have preferred to overlook. Social justice was an important social value for 14 per cent of citizens in 1990, at the beginning of the transition period. This proportion rose with reactions to the privatization process. Indeed, the question of social justice and the fairness of the privatization process has come to have a considerable influence on political parties, elections and ultimately, public policies. I will return to this issue later.

The early years of Croatia's transition saw a confrontation of inherited values with new or revived values, so that the social and political scene became polarized. At each pole was a set of basic values, one modern (individualism, Europeanization, secularism) and the other traditional (collective national identity, religious belief, conservative values in life). The polarization was reinforced by the nature and structure of party politics. The Croatian Democratic Union (CDU) has won all Croatian elections in the last seven years, showing itself to be the only political party able to win the majority required to form a non-coalition government. The opposition parties only have a chance of winning elections if they can form a successful opposition bloc, which has never happened so far. The political polarization is definable simply as the political force in power versus everybody else. Under this dominant political formula, the ruling party makes every effort to find cracks in any possible opposition alliances and drive wedges into them, which it has not been difficult to do. It only needs to fear a front-type opposition like the one that toppled the communists. Since its clear and unconditional victory in the first elections, the CDU has managed to retain a constant 45 per cent of the votes.

This, through a manufactured majority in Parliament, allows it to control the executive single-handedly.[6] Tudjman's party is more than a political organization. It started as a national movement encompassing all walks of Croatian life – urban and rural, young and old, men and women. Throughout the last seven years in power, this party or movement under Tudjman's authoritarian leadership has been reinforced by a centralized structure and backed by a reward system, whereby state and local-government positions are used to reward loyal and punish disloyal members of the rank and file. This soon produced a situation where the president controlled and managed the wheels of the party-state machine, and resulted in a political declaration of the "historic and natural relation" between the party and the state. In this, the CDU is declared to be the creator and sole guarantee of the state's survival. So an opposition electoral victory would ostensibly pose a danger of losing the state again to foreign powers or to former communist or federal neighbours. This kind of identification has added dramatically to the polarized interpretation of Croatian politics.

The opposition side of Croatian politics contains four to six political parties capable of exceeding the 5 per cent vote threshold to qualify for seats. They include parties of liberal, peasant, social-democrat, regional, Christian, and radical right ideological orientations, which strive to form effective coalitions with different combinations of partners for each election. This has produced constant changes on the opposition side of the Croatian Parliament. A different party or coalition has been the leading opposition force in each of three parliamentary terms. This fragmentation and instability have produced conditions in which the ruling party can easily win the single-member constituency seats under the plurality rule. It has also damaged the image of the opposition parties in the eyes of the voters (helped and encouraged by state-controlled television). Only the Social Democratic Party of Croatia (SDP), the reformed communists, has managed a steady rise in support, from 3 per cent of the vote in 1992, to 14 per cent in 1997. This growing popularity is hardly surprising considering the social conditions and consequences produced by the government's privatization policies.

The polarization is reinforced by the presidential elections, which by their nature present the electorate with two competing camps. The real decision facing the electorate is whether to vote for the incumbent or against him. One of the negative consequences of this domi-

Table 6.1 **Election turn-outs in Croatia**

Year	Type of election	Percentage of electorate voting
1990	First democratic parliamentary elections	84
1992	First presidential election	75
1992	Elections to House of Representatives	76
1993	Elections for House of Counties	64
1995	Elections to House of Representatives	69
1997	Elections for House of Counties	71
1997	Second presidential election	55

Note: The percentages were also affected by changes in electoral law, with the enfranchisement of Croatian citizens permanently resident outside the Republic of Croatia. The size of the electorate increased from 3,420,212 in 1990 to 4,070,032 in 1997.
Source: Data compiled from official election reports.

nance by the incumbent party and its candidates is that a mounting number of citizens prefer not to vote at all. This is clearly apparent in Table 6.1.

Participation in elections is one side of the important, wider issues of political participation as a precondition for a viable democratic system. Parties alone are not sufficient to provide a democratic process in which civil society is able to express, advance, and realize the interests of private owners. A recent poll showed that there is interest in participating in the democratic life of the community present in about half of respondents.[7] This applies not only as a general statement, but in their exposure to the media and political information, in discussion of public affairs in conversation, and in real knowledge of basic political information. One-third of the sample has no interest in politics. However, more than 80 per cent of those who have a satisfactory level of general political interest consider that they have little or no influence over local or national government. Since their political effectiveness is small and they see no chance of changing this by participation, they look upon voting as the maximum political activity they are prepared to show. The political culture of the transition period, with its institutional setting and social environment, does not favour political participation, so that people very seldom take any initiative to change a situation or solve a problem.[8] Underlying constraints on higher levels of political participation can be found in the nature of the political system, which is centralized and rigid, with limited opportunities for inputs and slow feedback mechanisms. On a systemic level, Croatia, like other post-communist countries, is undergoing a process of institutional stabilization. This is marked by heavy regulative activity and bureaucratic tendencies. Such stabilization processes, coupled with bureaucratic trends and strong centralization of the state apparatus, have blocked off the opportunities for individuals or groups to exert influence, which curbs their perception of influence and political efficacy. A strong political party in power limits individual political ambition outside the realm of party politics. Croatia's political life in general has been captured by the political parties (including the opposition parties). One might almost say it had been stolen from the citizens, due to the role parties have played in the transition period through the electoral process. Politics in Croatia is concentrated in intra-party and inter-party relations.

Stabilization of the political institutions does not automatically mean democratization of them. The perception of institutional stabilization is challenged by opposition parties and political scientists arguing for constitutional change: limits on the powers of the president, stronger checks and balances, stronger political influence for elected representatives, and more autonomy for local government. It is widely held that democratic institutions can still be altered at the will of powerful players. Democratic consolidation has not yet arrived in the sense of stabilized, structured democratic procedures and system maintenance. The process of national integration and state-building in times of war and national defence has had a decisive impact on the form and character of political institutions and the policy-making process. This is apparent in the privatization process, where it will have important long-term consequences on the distribution of social and political power, and the new structure of Croatian society, defining the winners and losers of post-communism. This was the kind of social and political environment in which the privatization process was devised and implemented.

Privatization: Public policy without the public

The Croatian government's early decision to start the privatization process cannot be understood only in terms of the standard economic explanations about the advantages and benefits of a market economy. There were some strategic political reasons as well. The first privatization legislation was passed in April 1991, a year after the CDU's electoral victory, while the country was still within the Federal state and some of the Serbian population was in open rebellion. Changing property rights by privatization and restructuring the basis of the economy was expected to achieve several political objectives:

117

- It would demonstrate to the European Community and others in the "West" the new government's determination to install capitalism and a Western type of economy. (The authorities maintained that the political system was already democratic and constitutional, based on the new Croatian Constitution of December 1990.)
- Privatization would distinguish the Croatian economy from the other Federal republics, and strengthen the grounds for state independence, once that issue came to the fore. It would also make it simpler to disentangle the Croatian economy from the Federal economic structures.
- Privatization would be the ultimate instrument for purging the economic sphere of communist influence. (In the event, communist managers were the only people around with the expertise to run the economy, and they showed remarkable skill in buying out the firms they managed.) Furthermore, the redistribution of economic wealth and power would help the new political élite to gain control over the real sources of power.
- Taking over the main sectors of the economy and declaring them state (as opposed to "social") property helped to stabilize the system and preserve asset values in turbulent times, while providing budget revenue for the state and the police and for building up the Croatian armed forces.

These and other objectives shaped the country's course of privatization. There were few alternatives, the reasoning was straightforward, and the decisions ensued quickly, with little public debate or discourse. Although economists as a profession debated alternative privatization models, such as rapid distribution of property among the population, there was little reflection of these polemics among the public or in the media, and even less among members of parliament or within the ruling party. Only five amendments were tabled to the bill. Even the prominent economist who advocated rapid distribution of shares to the general public began to defend revenue-oriented privatization wholeheartedly once he had been appointed the deputy prime minister in charge of economic policy.

The 1991 Act provided for two phases of privatization. The first was the "phase of autonomous privatization," in which existing firms (usually smaller ones with assets worth less than DM 5 million) drew up their own plans of privatization, which the state agency allowed or disallowed. The dominant forms of privatization at this stage were employee and manager buy-outs (EBO and MBO). Under EBO, employees could buy shares in instalments, on a sliding scale of dis-

Table 6.2 **Number of firms registered in Croatia, 1990–1993**

Year	Number of registered firms
1990	17,923
1991	32,900
1992	56,018
1993	83,345

Source: Slobodna Dalmacija (1994), Split, 14 January.

counts related to years of employment (a 20 per cent discount with an extra 1 per cent discount for each year of employment), up to a nominal value of DM 20,000. They also had first refusal on the rest of the shares being sold at full price.[9] Other forms used were public share issues and public auctions on the stock exchange. A total of 2,584 firms were privatized to 656,054 shareholders before the end of the first phase, on 30 June 1992. On that date, all firms not already privatized under the more relaxed procedures (usually larger companies) came under the control of the Croatian Privatization Fund (the CPF, owning two-thirds of them, with the pension fund owning the remaining third). The CPF was now able to privatize the firms under several different schemes and sets of rules. A group of so-called state companies has still not been privatized, and there is to be new legislation before this happens. These are in industries deemed to be of strategic importance, such as oil, electricity generation and distribution, railways, postal and telecommunication services, television, state forests, and roads.

The government played a direct role in the privatization process through the CPF, which had wide discretionary powers. Acting as a manager of state property, it had powers to sell companies, value them, appoint managers, monitor performance, terminate contracts with shareholders who failed to pay on time, and so on.

At the end of the first phase, public debate on the future of privatization was resumed, but with little success. The opposition parties were prevented in committee from placing the matter on the parliamentary agenda. Trade unions protested and called for voucher schemes of free privatization. Members of the public were more preoccupied with surviving the difficult times, and gave no attention or time to the murky and intricate procedures of becoming shareholders. There was no programme to educate the public or provide mass information, and few members of the public had spare money to

119

invest. So the 85 per cent preference for a give-away privatization programme is understandable. Meanwhile the first cases of abuse and malpractice became public. Yet all the ruling party would promise was more of the same type of privatization at a faster tempo. Croatia at the time was in the midst of war, with one-third of its territory occupied. There were UN peace-keeping forces in the country, and it was hardly a good time for big policy changes, especially not for any kind of give-away privatization scheme.[10] What was needed, however, was fresh capital. This the government hoped to obtain from the Croatian "diaspora" and from foreign investors.

New privatization legislation came into force on 1 March 1996. However, the political situation by then was very different from what it had been in 1991–1992. In the summer of 1995, the Croatian army had regained the occupied regions of Krajina from Serbian control. The eastern part of the country was transferred from Serbian occupation to a temporary UN administration, and was due to rejoin the Croatian state by 15 January 1998. Croatia had been a recognized member of the international community for four years.

The new laws introduced some new privatization procedures, but most of the techniques had already been employed earlier. The most important innovation was the "right to shares free of charge." At last Croatia had its own version of a mass privatization. However, the war entered the picture again, or rather its aftermath. The free shares were supposed to be issued (as coupons) to an estimated 300,000 victims of the war. (In the event, fewer than 200,000 have actually registered for coupons.)[11] The total value of the programme is DM 3.5 billion. It will include non-core activities of the national oil company and 30 per cent of Croatia Airlines. The remainder consists of a mixed bag of firms whose shares on the open market will probably be worth only about 40 per cent of their nominal value or less.

The new entrepreneurs

The situation in the country and the government's strategic political objectives limited the debate on privatization options. Croatia at war did not have a stable population. Some of the population were in rebellion, and many thousands were displaced by Serbian forces. Assets and the tax base were shrinking, so that a revenue-oriented privatization policy was a rational choice.

The incomplete legislation, the wide discretionary powers left to the state privatization authorities, the opaque rules, and the minimal monitoring of the process left privatization prone to malpractice and corruption. The limited transparency and parliamentary control allowed for favouritism, shady deals, a client system, and other deviant practices. Although most of these were not criminal acts, they were not socially equitable or morally correct. Some of the loopholes have been closed by the new legislation, but there has been no real effort made to curtail practices of this kind or stop political patronage and favours. The small political efforts made in this direction by the ruling party were simply part of its election campaigns.

On the other hand, it is fair to say that these problems were not great enough to justify the demand for an annulment of privatization and total revision of the process. Some opposition parties proposed that all privatization deals so far be reviewed, but the public was unsure about the consequences of such a course and whether it would benefit the stability of the country. The issue of social justice in privatization commands a high level of public support: 67 per cent agree that privatization has not been conducted fairly. However, it is hard to interpret this kind of redistribution in terms of social justice for all. Will there be benefits for the nation such as improved economic performance, more jobs and higher standards of living? Will civil society strengthen and social interests become structured? Those are the real tests of a privatization policy. So the issue of social justice will need to be re-evaluated.

Another social dimension of the new economic system, connected only marginally with the privatization process induced and controlled by the state, is "grassroots capitalism" – the considerable number of new private businesses. There is an emerging class of entrepreneurs, of thousands of self-employed owners of businesses, alongside the shareholders. This mushrooming of small business is continually influencing market behaviour, and challenging existing, inert companies, especially in the technologically advanced sectors. Being a capitalist is a new and welcome value in Croatian society. Business culture and values are also penetrating into the non-economic sector, putting new standards before bureaucrats and civil servants (cost, efficiency, payment of taxes, planning, courtesy, etc.) This all goes to show how economies in transition are necessarily social orders in transition as well.[12]

Privatization has strong links with several other agenda items in the transition period. Frequent changes of privatization rules, often with further injections of voluntarism, had negative effects on the general image of the legal system, and lessened confidence in legal stability and the rule of law. Meanwhile the cases of privatization-related patronage, favouritism, nepotism, abuse of power, insider trading, unfair lobbying, etc. have detrimentally affected political culture.

The CPF also sees privatization as a public policy with a wide spectrum of objectives, economic and social. It argues that privatization is not only about a change in property relations. It is also about helping war victims, displaced persons, and refugees, financing reconstruction of war-damaged areas, strengthening pension funds, stabilizing the banking system, restoring property to original owners, generating state revenue, enticing back emigrés, and attracting foreign investment.[13]

The high levels of uncertainty that characterize post-communist societies are exponentially higher when the country is under attack. While many analysts agree with the intended policy objectives, they are critical about how far they are being achieved. Privatization did not raise the expected quantity of revenue.[14] Firms were often sold at less than their market value, or failed to find a buyer, so that they were transferred to the control of the pension funds. The pension funds own shares with a nominal value of DM 54.5 million, but in most cases this is merely on paper, and the securities have a very low real resale value. The dividends earned from these shares make no impression on personal pensions. Because of the high risks, foreign direct investment (DM 470 million so far) and even the diaspora capital (about DM 160 million) have been slow to make a serious commitment to Croatia.

Democracy and privatization

The standard debate about the speed, timing, and forms of economic transition in post-communist societies was not considered a decisive issue in Croatia. State-controlled, revenue-oriented privatization and later legislative decisions about privatization were mainly determined by wider regional processes: the collapse of Yugoslavia and the subsequent wars in Croatia and Bosnia-Herzegovina, and the type of political force that took over. These developments tended to overshadow the dominant subjects in other ex-socialist countries – democratization, privatization, and social change.

The strategic objectives chosen for the privatization policy in Croatia were not primarily targeted at strengthening democratization or civil society. Privatization and the economic transition were associated only secondarily with democracy as their underlying social base. *Privatization has taken place under the pressure of war and its consequences, which has blurred the conceptual link between democracy and the market.* No systemic correlation between privatization and democratization can be clearly discerned, at least not for the first five or six years.[15]

There is no unconditional answer to the question of the legitimacy of privatization and popular support for it, and especially of public willingness to bear economic hardship. The legitimacy of the new political élite and the CDU is related not only to victories in competitive elections, but to the processes of state-building and national defence. Mass mobilization against the new regime, based on the economic transition, was not feasible. Not even the moral problem of new "big capitalists" (yesterday's truck driver an owner of a major industry today) and whether they deserve their new-found wealth, or the common feeling of social injustice ("We fought at the front while 'they' got rich"), could mobilize mass protests.

Seven years on, with the wars behind them, citizens are reorienting their attention to a new set of issues and priorities. The first indication of this reorientation came in November 1996, with mass demonstrations supporting an independent radio station in Zagreb. This was the first protest on such a scale against a decision by the new democratic government, and demonstrated the truism of democracy that government is not identical to the state.

Croatian citizens are coming to realize that much of the privatization had already happened while they had other concerns. Trade unions, political parties, and other non-governmental organizations are voicing dissatisfaction with the privatization results and consequences, as part of their efforts to recruit members and supporters. The media print privatization scandals about what went on a few years ago. Political scientists will conclude that a *desirable balance between state interests, economic efficiency, and social equity has not been accomplished.* The order of priorities was state interests first, economic objectives second, and social equity last. The current attempt to alter these priorities by distributing free coupons will do little or nothing to remedy the situation. Privatization is being used again for an extraneous purpose, to quell dissatisfaction among those who lost and suffered most in the war, instead of the privatization process being speeded up, as economic rationality demands.

Privatization is returning to Croatia's national agenda in the indirect form of economic indicators, standard of living, and basic problems of salaries and employment. Two-thirds of citizens, when asked what are the main problems in Croatia today, list a problem in the economic field: unemployment (24 per cent), the economic situation (11 per cent), individual economic position (10 per cent) standard of living (13 per cent), or the consequences of the war (10 per cent). General political issues of democratic development, human rights, and the political system come far behind.

This gives a strong message about how citizens view the national agenda. The performance on these sets of problems will influence the political side of the agenda and the way it develops. The legitimacy of the transition depends closely on the performance of the privatized economy. The members of the political élite are slowly realizing the political cost of the economic transition. Blind to the social consequences of "wild capitalism," they counted on other sources of popularity and electoral support (war and the dangers to the integrity of the state). It is now clear that exposing citizens to the cold winds of the market while reducing their social protection had to evoke some kind of backlash. This is apparent in the rising vote for the SDP, which has become the strongest opposition party, associated in people's minds with the role of a real opposition. It did not come as a surprise when an SDP-led opposition coalition won by a big margin in local election reruns in December 1997, in Primorsko-Goranska County (round Rijeka). To link collective decisions about the choice of government with issues of economic performance and personal standard of living is a slow, time-consuming process that tests government effectiveness and the stability of the democratic environment – above all the assurance that those who lose actually step down from office. This is something Croatian citizens need to work on in the remaining years of the millennium.

Notes

1. A similar thesis is advanced by Vojmir Franičević: "We shall argue that many peculiarities of Croatian privatization (e.g. low respect for formal rules, methods of sale, partial renationalization, etc.) stem from the specific choices made by the new political élite and from certain hard facts about the war-time Croatian society and economy." See Franičević, Vojmir (1997), "Privatization in Croatia: Developments and Issues," paper presented to the 29th National Convention of the American Association for the Advancement of Slavic Studies, Seattle, 20–23 November, ms., p. 2.
2. The analysis here employs Theodore Lowi's classification of policy redistributive, regulative, and distributive types. See Lowi, Theodore (1964), "American Business, Public Policy, Case Studies and Political Theory," *World Politics*, Vol.

16, pp. 677–715. A similar classification appears in Offe, Claus (1991), "Capitalism by Democratic Design? Democratic Theory Facing the Triple Transition in East Central Europe," *Social Research*, Vol. 58, No. 4, pp. 864–892.

3. On the incomplete nature of the collapse of the state socialism, see Bunce, Valerie (1993), "A 'Transition to Democracy'?" *Contention*, Vol. 3, No. 1, pp. 34–47. On the importance of legacies from the former regime (self-management and programmes of economic reform) in producing "sensitivity to the path of privatization," see also Franičević (1997), p. 6.

4. The items have been paraphrased. For the originals, see *Delegatski vjesnik*, No. 510, 7 July 1990, p. 6. For more on the items, see Grdešić, Ivan (1998), "Building the State: Actors and Agendas," in Ivan Šiber (ed.), *The 1990 and the 1992/93 Sabor Elections in Croatia*, Berlin: Wissenschaftszentrum Berlin fur Sozialforschung.

5. All the survey data presented in this study come from pre-election polls with representative samples, conducted in 1990, 1992, 1995, and 1997 by the research team engaged in the project "Elections, Parties and Parliament in Croatia: 1990–2000," based at the Faculty of Political Science, University of Zagreb. The author is the coordinator of this team.

6. The CDU gained an average of 7–10 per cent more seats than its percentage of the votes in the proportional representation part of the elections. With the plurality part of the election, the discrepancy is almost 50 per cent. This means it gains a majority of the seats with only a plurality of the votes.

7. The sample of 1,000 respondents in six cities was polled in April 1997.

8. The Public Participation (PP) Index is composed of four sets of data: general interest, perception of influence, perception of possible change in PP, and willingness to participate in election campaigns. This produces an aggregate average measure of participation.

9. For more detail, see Bićanić, Ivo (1993), "Privatization in Croatia," *East European Politics and Society*, Vol. 7, No. 3, pp. 422–439.

10. The main architect of the privatization programme was the Croatian deputy prime minister in charge of the economy, Borislav Škegro. He commented as follows on that period: "Without any reservations, 1993, 1994, and 1995 were great years for the implementation of radical reforms. First, we had the absolute support of the president, and the security [of knowing] that if there was going to be trouble, it would pass through Parliament. Secondly, we had authority at that time to issue decrees with legislative force. We had free hands. We had the political will, the support and the means to do the job." *Tjednik*, 29 March 1997, p. 26.

11. Qualifying categories: displaced persons and refugees, military personnel wounded in war, families of fallen, imprisoned, or missing soldiers, former Croatian prisoners of war, military personnel disabled in non-wartime conditions, families of civilians killed, interned, or missing, Croatian civilians still interned after 19 September 1997, civilians disabled in wartime, unemployed persons previously employed in occupied territory, former political prisoners.

12. Bunce, Valerie (1993), "Leaving Socialism: A Transition to Democracy?" *Contention*, Vol. 3, No. 1, pp. 34–47.

13. See *Privatizacija u Hrvatskoj: Izvješće o privatizaciji – do 1. siječnja 1997. godine* (1997), Zagreb: Hrvatski fond za privatizaciju, veljača.

14. Bičanić, Ivo (1995), "Political Repercussions of Denationalization and Privatization in the Context of Croatia's Transition," paper presented at the conference "The Transition to Democracy in South-eastern Europe: The Case of Croatia," Lovran, 6 September 1995, ms, p. 6.
15. As Leonard J. Cohen writes, "The impact of privatization on the overall division of political and economic power in Croatia served to reinforce tendencies toward elite control by those associated with the new ruling party." See Cohen (1997), "Embattled Democracy: Post-communist Croatia in Transition," in Karen Dawisha and Bruce Parrot (eds.), *Politics, Power and the Struggle for Democracy in South-east Europe*, Cambridge: Cambridge University Press, p. 90.

7

Political and economic factors in the democratic transformation of Slovakia: Achievements and problems

Ján Morovic

The key factors of democratic transformation

The problems that relate to the interactions between the political and economic changes in Slovakia's transformation process have two dimensions. The first applies to all countries in transition from a centrally planned, socialist system to a market system and derives from their initial level of economic development and other economic characteristics. Slovakia was a relatively developed middle-level industrial country in 1989. Its agriculture made it 92 per cent self-sufficient in food and other agricultural commodities.

The second dimension applies not only to Slovakia, but to Ukraine, the Czech Republic, and some other countries. It relates to the task of establishing a new state. This entails changes to the existing institutional system, and the establishment of a new legal and institutional framework. For example, when a new state is established the transformation of the legislative system provides an opportunity to move towards the legislative systems of developed countries in Europe and elsewhere in the world. Naturally, the process of becoming an independent state also carries some risks. These include a reduction in the size of the domestic market, increased vulnerability to crime and national security risks, a shortage of experts who were not based in the country gaining independence, and so on.

These considerations not only influence economic development, which is in essence part of the transformation, but alse components of the systemic change such as ownership patterns and privatization. The process of "voucher" privatization that had started in Czechoslovakia was discontinued in Slovakia after independence, but management-instigated privatization continued. There has been a strong link between political and economic processes in subsequent years.

The Slovak Republic came into existence on 1 January 1993 through a division conducted in a constitutional and politically civilized fashion. However, the split had several detrimental effects on the Slovak economy. This was the first time that Slovakia had existed as an independent state, apart from a brief period of limited independence during the Second World War. Slovakia is undergoing a process of search for its identity as a state. This complicates the vital process of integrating the country into overall European and world structures (for example the EU and NATO). Slovakia's situation in this respect is symptomatic of a dilemma facing Europe at large, with two opposing, or perhaps only seemingly opposing, trends of integration and devolution appearing at once.

Slovakia's historical position defines or affects various aspects of its development. Politically and economically it shows a measure of authoritarianism. This is attributable to the evolving political cultivation of a new state, and from the decrease of living standards and social security experienced by some sections of the population. These authoritarian tendencies upset the balance between the executive, legislative, and judicial branches of the state. Also central to the country's concurrent processes of identification and integration is the question of minority rights, which is an essential factor in democratic transformation both domestically and in international relations. Although minority rights are a problematic issue for a young state in the process of establishing its identity, they are essential to Slovakia's integration into European structures.

In the economic sphere the gradual separation from the Czech Republic was a basic issue for the new state. After 1993 Slovakia had to define an economic strategy of its own, carefully considering the country's specific features. The separation was followed by a period of stabilization that prevented devaluation and inflation, and protected the requirements for economic growth. This was partly caused by the restrictive policies of the central bank (National Bank of

Slovakia). Another key move was the introduction of import and exchange charges. These influenced the trends in the balance of trade and payments, and increased the competitiveness of Slovak exports, which began to be reoriented towards the markets of developed countries.

It is possible to say that by the beginning of 1997, the Slovak Republic had successfully completed the introductory stabilization period in its transformation process. Recently, the focus has shifted from the macroeconomic to the microeconomic plane as the economy passes through an intensive process of restructuring, due to declining performance and competitiveness. This shift is associated with the social dimension of the country's democratic transformation. The low wage costs and high educational qualifications of the labour force are an important factor in economic development, contributing to competitiveness and helping to attract foreign direct investment (FDI). However, the population has also had to cope with a sharp fall in the standard of living (by more than 30 per cent) while witnessing a rapid differentiation in personal wealth. The social problems, including high unemployment in some regions, may lead to levels of dissatisfaction with economic policy and the government that complicate the democratization process.

Political factors: The constitution and the realities

The constitution of the Slovak Republic, which was approved by the National Council in 1992, laid the basis for the democratic transformation of independent Slovakia. Implementation of its provisions is essential to successfully continuing the democratization process. The constitution is based on both the national and the civil principles that have proved decisive to the democratic transformation of Slovakia. It guarantees the rights of minorities and other ethnic groups, in agreement with international norms applied in Europe. The main principles of the constitution have been tested in practice in the last five years. They cover the rule of law, the sovereignty of citizens, the triple division of state power, the priority of legal standards, and the equality and inviolable character of property.

In principle, the political structure of the new Slovak state has been shaped by the new constitution. The constitution defines the Slovak Republic as a parliamentary democracy, and also provides a useful framework for discussing the political factors involved in the democratic transformation. The political realities of every country have to be related on one hand to the constitution and on the other hand to those political factors and forces which shape the realities, which implement or disregard the basic law of their countries.

According to the constitution, the parliament is the central legislative institution of the state, with a vital role in the democratization process. Known as the National Council of the Slovak Republic, the legislature consists of a single chamber with 150 members elected for a four-year term on a basis of proportional representation. Seats are distributed among the parties receiving at least 5 per cent of the valid votes cast. The existence of a truly plural system is apparent from the large number of political formations (79 registered parties). Parties that gained more than 3 per cent of the vote in the previous general elections can claim state funding. The president of the Republic can dissolve the National Council if there is a vote of no confidence in the government three times within six months after the elections. Apart from that, it may only be dissolved if two-thirds of its members vote to do so.

The Slovak Republic is divided administratively into eight regions and 79 districts, headed by representatives of public administration. An act passed in July 1996 expanded the jurisdiction of these bodies and diminished that of local government. The distribution of responsibilities between the decentralized levels of state government and local government is still not wholly clarified. The administration does not operate under legislation that clearly defines the rights and responsibilities of state employees, which complicates the struggle against corruption.

The elections, which took place in September 1994, brought to power a coalition government led by the Movement for a Democratic Slovakia (Hnutie za demokraticke Slovensko). This government, which has been replaced after the elections in 1998 by a democratic coalition, was strongly criticized by a growing segment of the population and also by some international organizations for a number of reasons. A survey undertaken in 1996, by the Institute for the Survey of Public Opinion, indicated that the public placed decreasing trust in the existing institutions. Respondents pinpointed several concerns (listed in order of frequency): living standards, social security, unemployment, the critical state of democracy, the observation of the law, criminality, and the economy. The responses marked a considerable decline in the voters' confidence in the government but on the whole the responses were much influenced by respondents' party loyalties and preferences.

Popular concerns about the state of democracy increased. According to research by Eurobarometer, 67 per cent of respondents in 1995 expressed such concerns, whereas the proportion was 74 per cent a year later. More respondents thought that individual human rights were not respected in Slovakia (the ratio increased from 51 per cent in 1995 to 58 per cent in 1996). The surveys also revealed that an increasing number of respondents thought politicians were not interested in or influenced by popular opinion, and that the political scene was not transparent enough. Politics were of peripheral interest to over half the sample (56 per cent). The internal discontent was paralleled by the external critical statements.

A study of the European Union in 1997 rated as unacceptable the procedures under which the parliament operated. It criticized the lack of respect for the opposition shown by the government and the majority members. During the period from September 1994 to January 1997, the opposition had no chance of gaining adequate representation on the parliamentary committees for control and investigation, responsible for monitoring the secret service and the armed forces information service. These committees have not been convened because the government refused to accept opposition candidates for membership in them. Reactions to this from abroad, particularly from the European Union, had much influence on public opinion, because of the growing popular wish for becoming a member both of the EU and of NATO.

The constitution guarantees many civil and political rights: accessibility of recourse to legal action, protection from unauthorized arrest, the right to vote for those over 18, the right of assembly, and respect for personal privacy. Slovakia has signed the Geneva agreement on refugees, and foreign nationals seeking asylum are protected by internationally guaranteed rights and safeguards.

The government had considerable influence over the public broadcast media, so that there has been a marked imbalance between government and opposition media access. However, the growing private sector (1 private national and 5 local television companies and 20 private radio stations) has brought a considerable expansion of freedom of the press. This trend has been supported by access to a growing number of foreign television and radio stations (49 licences for cable broadcasting).

The press is remarkably varied (11 national dailies and 7 others distributed in more than one region), although the pro-government daily *Slovenska Republika* receives considerable public funding.

The Slovak Republic has accepted several norms for respect for basic human and minority rights. The international agreements to which Slovakia, a member of the Council of Europe since June 1993, has signed include the European Agreement on Human Rights and its main appendices, signed by Czechoslovakia in March 1992. This confers on private individuals the right of recourse to the European Court in case of alleged encroachment on their rights under that agreement. Slovakia has endorsed other international agreements on the protection of human rights and the rights of minorities, including the Agreement on the Elimination of Torture, and the Framework Agreement on Minorities. It has also endorsed the main agreements of the UN on human rights. There has been a problem with minority rights.

Of Slovakia's 5.3 million inhabitants, 18–23 per cent belong to minorities, of which the largest are the Hungarians (11 per cent) and the Gypsies or Romanies (estimates vary from 4.8 per cent to 10 per cent). In all new countries that remain multi-ethnic, the relations between the national group establishing the state and the other national groups stay or become a complex process. They incorporate several dimensions – political, legal, institutional, social, and economic. This applies to Slovakia, where finding an appropriate solution in a democratic way that satisfies all needs is a long-term process calling for a carefully considered government strategy and appropriate development of the legislative system, through cooperation between government and parliament. Historical richness of development within the establishing nation and development in cooperation with other nations' communities should provide a positive basis for multi-cultural development in the whole of Central Europe. Conflicts and problems come about mainly for want of tolerance and magnanimity in resolving problems that are not usually very extensive.

The constitution guarantees minorities the right to cultural development, the reception of information and education in their own language, and participation in decision-making that concerns them. Although representation of the minorities in parliament is not regulated by special legislation, the Hungarian minority has held 17 seats since the 1994 elections. The state budget allots funds to support minority cultural and educational activities.

There are a number of international norms guaranteeing protection of minorities. In September 1995, Slovakia ratified the Framework Agreement of the Council of Europe on the rights of minorities.

However, it did not accept Recommendation 1201 of the Parliamentary Assembly of the European Council, which lays down the collective rights of minorities and is not legally binding. The Agreement on Friendship and Cooperation with Hungary was signed in March 1995. It was ratified by the Slovak Parliament in March 1996 with two accompanying declarations, in which it refused to acknowledge the collective rights of minorities and denied the possibility of forming autonomous administrative structures on the basis of nationality. Although the Slovak Republic has followed the recommendations of the European Council on surnames and local names (allowing minority-language forms to be used), the use of a minority language is still not possible in a comprehensive legal document. Although the Hungarians and the rest of Slovakia's population coexist peacefully, these unresolved issues lead to some tension between the government and the minority. Consequently, many members of the public, Hungarian and Slovak, express increasing disagreement with government policy towards this minority.

A very important force in the struggle for the fulfilment of the democratic provisions in the constitution has been the NGO movement. There are almost 10,000 NGOs (associations of citizens or foundations) registered since 1990. However, many of these only have few members or seem to be inactive. The active ones deal with a range of concerns and activities (humanitarian, charitable, social, environmental, educational, cultural, human and minority rights, youth, sports, etc.)

The NGOs have been developing self-confidence and an awareness that they are part of a unique sector alongside the government and business sectors. They are developing contacts and strengthening cooperation with each other. Major groups of NGOs have entered into coalitions or umbrella organizations, such as the Slovak Humanitarian Council, Slovak Catholic Charity, Slovak Youth Council, Tree of Life, and others. The NGO movement in Slovakia, as in many other former socialist countries has been encouraged and supported, especially financially, by Western foundations and organizations. The first to provide assistance were private foundations, which remain the largest providers of indirect or direct assistance to such organizations in Slovakia. Obviously the further development of NGOs in Slovakia depends greatly on political and economic developments, but it will also require continued Western involvement and assistance. The sector is still fragile, and even the most dedicated citizens' organizations find it difficult to continue the work they have begun so well. Western assistance is needed as they seek to develop their programmes and build up their finances and human resources.

The 1998 elections brought about radical changes into the political life of Slovakia. There is a clear parliamentary majority which supports the democratization process, the re-establishing of democratic conditions within the parliament and in the country. They created a chance for representation in different parliamentarian positions for oppositions and coalitions according to the result of the elections (this was not the case in the previous four years). The Slovak Democratic Coalition (SDC) is a new party developed from five different parties with different political orientations, and its common creed is to re-establish democratic development within Slovakia. This party finished in second place at the previous elections. The first-placed Meciars' party (Movement for a Democratic Slovakia) was not able to create a new government. The SDC in coalition with the Slovak Democratic Left Party, the Hungarian minority party (Hungarian Coalition Party) and with a new party called the Party of Civil Comprehension created a new government.

The parliament was created in a proportional way. The chairman of the parliament was from the third strongest party – the Slovak Democratic Left Party. A new government was elected by the parliament with the participation of the representatives of the largest ethnic minority, the Hungarians.

The establishment of a market economy in Slovakia

The establishment of a market economy has been accelerated with the process of establishing an independent republic. Significant progress has been achieved on introducing legislation related to the new state structure. The reform of the legal system was directed towards the adoption of laws in which would be harmony with the European Union's single market, such as company law, banking, free movement of capital and taxation. With the help of macroeconomic stabilization programmes and loans and stand-by credits provided by international institutions, including the IMF, the World Bank, and the EC Phare programme, Slovakia managed to stabilize its economy, especially the domestic market.

Institutional changes

Price liberalization has reached a stage where only a few items still have controlled prices, such as heat, electricity, gas, petrol, water, some basic foodstuffs, pharmaceuticals, housing rents, the telephone service, and public transportation. The proportion of turnover of price-controlled items is only about 5 per cent of the total.

Trade liberalization has also reached an advanced stage. There are export restrictions only on some special products, and licensing procedures for a few commodities. Standard methods of protecting the domestic market such as certification and source-country specification are used.

Privatization in Slovakia has diverged from the methods applied in the Czech Republic and some other transition countries in Central Europe. Voucher privatization has ceased and privatization methods have been confined almost entirely to forms of direct sale. Privatization began in 1991 with the small-scale privatization of small firms, shops, and service providers, by public auction. During 1992 and 1993, the first stage of voucher privatization transferred property worth SKK 80 billion into private hands. Instead of voucher privatization, National Property Fund (NPF) bonds are to be used to sell shares in privatized enterprises.

The target for the second wave of privatization was to transfer assets worth about SKK 200 billion. However, the NPF altered the system of privatization. This meant that the voucher system and its associated investment funds were replaced by state interest-bearing bonds. In June 1995, the 3.5 million voucher holders were each compensated with an SKK 10,000 interest-bearing bond with a five-year term.

Small-scale privatization, in which domestic entrepreneurs were allowed to participate, was less significant in terms of the volume of property privatized. The entire process was conducted independently of the NPF. It covered the sale of about 10,000 units in 1993, worth a total of SKK 12 billion. Large-scale privatization was more significant. In the first wave, 678 enterprises with a combined value of SKK 169 billion were offered to foreign and domestic businesses and individuals. The second wave covered another 549 enterprises with the total value of SKK 258 billion.

The government excluded from privatization 29 companies, mainly in the energy industry, post and telecommunications, transport, water management, insurance and banking, to a total value of SKK 100 billion. The government also has a right of veto over the sale of another 12 companies classified as strategic.

From decline to growth

Separation from the Czech economy and the collapse of the Eastern markets resulted in a recession in the Slovak Republic: GDP decreased by a quarter between 1989 and 1993. Even in 1993 GDP decreased by 4 per cent, but then came a spectacular turnaround in 1994. The decline in living standard was about 30 per cent since 1990. Recovery began in a stable macroeconomic environment. GDP, at SKK 182 billion, was 4.8 per cent up on the previous year and equal in volume to GDP in 1991. This was mainly due to higher exports to EU countries and the Czech Republic. The improvement in macro-economic performance that started in 1994 continued and intensified in 1995, when GDP increased by 7.4 per cent. The same year scored the biggest rise in industrial productivity (8.4 per cent) and the lowest inflation rate (6 per cent), while the trade balance remained positive and the government deficit declined significantly. This was followed by a GDP increase of 6.9 per cent in 1996 and 6.5 per cent in 1997 with the private sector accounting for 76.8 per cent of the total. The GDP increase was mainly due to growth in the service sector.

Industry, especially heavy industry and the processing of raw materials, was the key sector of the independent Slovak economy, with a share in gross output of 47 per cent. During the transforma-tion, the share of industry in the production of GDP has been decreasing (to about 37 per cent in 1995). The growth rate of indus-trial output declined from 7.5 per cent in 1995 to 2.0 per cent in 1997. The growth of industrial chemicals and pharmaceuticals, which were the main standard-bearers of Slovakia's economic revival, declined rather fast due to sluggish demand for their products, mainly on for-eign markets. Metallurgy, which is among the essential export indus-tries representing about a quarter of total industrial exports also has growth problems.

The industry suffers from market disintegration, low competitive-ness on domestic and foreign markets, and slow progress with privati-zation and company transformation. Engineering is marked by excess capacity (suitable for a country of 40 million inhabitants), out-of-date technology, and an insufficiently flexible range of products.

The prospects for industrial development depend on several factors connected with markets (especially abroad), the economic environment, and continued economic transformation. The diversification of the Slovak economy away from the predominance of heavy industry is a necessary but difficult task.

Many enterprises are only beginning the process of restructuring and will need to modernize their equipment and methods. The main reasons for the sluggish restructuring have been constant state intervention, the weak banking sector, ineffective competition, and inadequate FDI.

The past five years have seen a complicated transformation process in agriculture, accompanied by market problems and financial crises. A decline in domestic spending and difficulties of access to solvent foreign markets, coupled with a shortage of capital, have caused a decline in agricultural production amounting to 25–30 per cent since 1989. The productivity of livestock farming decreased by half. This was caused mainly by an insufficiently prepared agricultural reform. Between 1989 and 1994 production costs rose by about 150 per cent and consumer prices by 70–80 per cent, while wholesale prices for agricultural products rose by only 50 per cent.

The government took a range of short and long-term measures designed to resolve the situation. The most significant was the agricultural programme adopted by parliament in 1993. The decline in agriculture has ceased. Whereas in 1992 almost 90 per cent of agricultural enterprises were on the verge of insolvency, in 1994 almost half the firms and a third of the state-owned enterprises in the sector made a profit.

The positive results show that the decisions by the government aimed at gradual stabilization in this sector were correct. In basic commodities, food quality and safety standards were maintained and the domestic market is becoming balanced and self-sufficient in agricultural products. However, for long-term stability, agriculture will require further structural changes and improvements in production parameters.

Slovakia has been successful in its macroeconomic and financial management. Restrictive macroeconomic policies have been used to help reduce inflation. The rate fell from almost 25 per cent in 1993, to 13.4 per cent in 1994, and has continued to ease. In 1995 it was 9.9 per cent, and in 1997 only 6.1 per cent, which meant that Slovakia had the lowest level of inflation in any of the transition countries. The inflationary pressure was relieved by the growth of GDP. The foreign-exchange stocks of the central bank and commercial banks also contributed considerably to decreasing inflation.

The average nominal wage in Slovakia was US$ 257 a month in 1996. There was a decline in the growth of real wages in 1997, compared to the earlier years, still, consumption was boosted primarily by increased domestic demand. Labour productivity rose by 4.4 per cent in 1997 compared with 2.4 per cent in 1996.

At the beginning of the transformation process, unemployment in the Slovak Republic was rising much faster than in the Czech Republic. This was because of higher dependence on Comecon markets and reliance on imports of cheap energy and raw materials from the former Soviet Union. This persistently high rate of unemployment is the economy's gravest problem. Over half of those without jobs are long-term unemployed, out of work for at least six months. The rate of registered unemployment in recent years has reached relatively high levels. In 1996 it was 12.8 per cent, in 1997 12.5 per cent, according to the methodology of the International Labour Organization. Regional differences are significant. The rate is highest in the southern and south-eastern regions of the country. The number of the long-term unemployed has significantly increased, while unemployment among young people is high and shows no tendency to fall.

The most obvious social achievement of the transformation is the formation of two public institutions: the Social Insurance Company (Socialna Poistovna) and the National Labour Bureau (Narodny urad prace). At present, the state considerably influences the operation of these, but as the differentiation of interests between employers and trade unions continues, the efforts towards greater autonomy for these institutions will increase.

Social policy-making also shows numerous problems, notably the fragmented, narrowly focused attempts to solve major problems. This brings frequent policy changes and reflects the differing interests of the government and the general public. Small businesses are protesting, in effect, against a system that inhibits the growth of the small-business sector by avoiding payment of the inordinately high insurance contributions.

The Slovak capital market started to develop shortly after the end of the first wave of voucher privatization. However, it was not established on a market-economy basis, because the underlying impulse came from the enormous offer of stock from the privatization process and not from the need of enterprises for investment funds. The authorities have been gradually relaxing certain restrictions on capital movement.

At the end of 1997 the official reserves stood at US$ 3.2 billion which was about eight times more than the central-bank reserves in January 1993, but both gross and net external debt increased rather fast.

After 41 years of communist planning, Slovakia has finally developed a functioning market economy and had attracted an FDI stock of over US$ 1 billion by 1997. It is relatively small, however, compared with the Czech Republic, about one-quarter the size. The low level of FDI was due to uncertainty over the Slovak government and its market and privatization-oriented reforms. Other negative factors were the difficulty of obtaining relevant information, the bureaucratic system, and shortcomings in legislation.

Lack of domestic finance is currently restricting investment growth, which fails to meet the restructuring needs of the economy and the growth in investment demand. The greatest amount of foreign investment has gone to industry, commerce, and the financial and insurance systems. Unfortunately none of this has been strategic, and it has not made a big contribution to restructuring the Slovak economy. The largest foreign investor is Germany, followed by Austria, the Czech Republic, the United States, France, the Netherlands, Sweden, the UK, and Italy.

The socio-economic and political transformation, in spite of the relatively small size of the country, also has its regional dimensions. Analysis of regional differences reveals differences of historical development in the political, economic, cultural, and ethnic spheres, and in the whole dimension of social change. There are regions dominated by agriculture, so that the transformation proceeds more slowly, because the development of agriculture is closely linked with the development of rural areas, and suffering from lack of finance. Other regions bear marks of strong reliance on heavy industry, and the problem is a shortage of alternative employment. One would expect a dramatic increase in small to medium-sized firms. This will require a strong, proactive policy for overall development of the business sector.

The new government in Slovakia intends to implement a long-term strategic programme, which would accelerate the modernization process and the structural transformation of the economy and implement the necessary correction in economic and social policies.

Conclusions

Even a preliminary evaluation of the democratization process and its interrelations with economic transformation must also be related to the complex institutional and even psychological aspects of establishing a new state. This process, which has been going on in Europe for centuries in all countries, including Slovakia, has many positive aspects, but it includes a number of complex problems. The changes and the interactions between them depend on the behaviour of political parties and the executive and legislative systems, and to some extent on international factors. This causes an interplay of various interests and values. It may produce results that conflict with the postulates of one or other aspects of the transition process, such as the building of a democratic civil society, the new role of the state, and the mutual relations between the pillars of democracy and the integration of the country into the global economy. Synchronizing the processes of nation-building with democratization and market development presents an extremely difficult set of tasks. Accomplishment of them requires a systemic approach, with constant analysis of the emerging political, economic, and social problems and tensions to facilitate the identification of appropriate corrective measures and changes. The elections in 1998 created more favourable conditions in Slovakia for realizing those tasks.

References

Agenda 2000 (1997), *Agenda 2000: Posudok Komisie k ziadosti Slovenska o clenstvo v Europskej unii* (Agenda 2000: The Committee Judgement Concerning the Application of Slovakia for EU Membership), Bratislava: Slovak Government.

Business Central Europe (1997), issues of February, August.

Butora, Martin, ed. (1997), *Slovensko 1996: Suhrnna sprava o stavespolocnosti a trendoch na rok 1997.*

A Comprehensive Report on the State of Society and Trends for the Year 1997 (1998), Bratislava: Institut pre verejne otazky.

Chovanec, Jan (1996), *Path to the Sovereignty of the Slovak Republic*, Bratislava: SIA.

EC (1996), *European Economy*, Supplement C, Nos. 1, 3, 10, and 11, October/ November, Luxembourg: Office for Official Publications of the European-Community.

EU (1996), *EU Questionnaire for the Slovak Republic*, Bratislava: Slovak Information Agency.

ING (1997), *Slovakia Capital and Money Market Report*, Amsterdam: ING Bank NV.

Karasz, P., J. Rencko, and I. Pauhofova (1997), *Economic Potential of the Regions of Slovakia from the Viewpoint of their Development Possibilities*, Bratislava: Monitor.

Monitor of the Economy of the Slovak Republic, Part 2, No. 3, Bratislava: Statistical Report (1996).

Statistical Annual Report 1996, *The Slovak Republic*, Bratislava.

Statistical Review (1996), *Statistical Review of the Slovak Republic*, No. 4, Bratislava.

Statistical Yearbook (1996), *Statistical Yearbook of the Slovak Republic*, Bratislava.

US Department of Commerce (1995), *Country Commercial Guide to The Slovak Republic*, October, American Business Centre.

8

The changing political system and realities in Hungary

Kálmán Kulcsár

Although Hungary, during its modern history, usually possessed institutions incorporating some elements of democracy, it was not a democratic country in the classical sense. The establishment of a modern, democratic political system after the end of "socialist" rule was a radical alteration, but not without precedent in Hungarian history. This return to a multi-party system recalled, for instance, the post-war political structure in the second half of the 1940s, and in some respects the political milieu of the inter-war period.

So one cannot ignore the country's traditions, experience, and political cultivation when exploring, for instance, how far the new political system can handle society's conflicts and resolve its economic and social problems democratically, or whether the transition may produce conditions that jeopardize consolidation of the democratic system.

The Hungarian political system, like others, functions in a socio-economic environment of which political traditions and cultivation form only one component. Another set of constituent conditions consists of the economic processes, and the global and regional aspects and the social consequences of them. These factors are especially important to the democratization process and the changes in the political system, because of the dual purpose behind the transition. The changes in all the "new democracies" are greatly influenced by the construction of a market economy, which necessarily causes special-interest groups to proliferate and increases the chance that they will aspire to influence or even combat the democratic process. It may also create a situation in which democracy loses political legitimacy. So the situation is ambivalent: successful economic reform is a *basic requirement* of political consolidation, but defending its efficacy produces tensions that *impede* political consolidation.

This makes it especially important for the political system to possess an accurate feedback mechanism, through all the organizations and individuals that affect the flow of information between the system and its environment. Only by studying the political system in conjunction with that feedback mechanism can one arrive at an answer to the questions put at the beginning.

The Hungarian legislation that shaped the change of political system in 1989–1990 (including Act XXXI 1989 that radically amended the constitution), was a reform introduced from the top down. Although the parliament realized that the public supported the changes, it legislated on the basis of a consensus between the ruling-party élite, represented by the government, and the emerging élite of the opposition parties. Since then, these legal norms have been legitimized politically by two general elections and by the rulings of the Constitutional Court.

During the early stages of the transition, the legal framework of the political system rested mainly on an interpretation of liberal ideas assumed to be rational. This was linked with social reality by the party interests, mistrust, fears, and suspicions (concealed ambitions) arising from the political situation at the time. This had deficiencies:
- there was no assessment made of how the real model of liberal representative democracy functions in the developed countries;
- also lacking was an assessment of the situation and political cultivation of Hungarian society. This should have covered knowledge and political skills, experience and cultivation of organizations and individuals embodying the emerging political system, and past experience with Hungarian political systems, especially traditions of Hungarian parliamentarianism, and several other factors.

Despite this criticism, it can be stated that a liberal, democratic institutional set-up was optimal and probably *essential* for successful transformation of the Central and Eastern European (CEE) societies as they emerged from autocracy. (It should be remembered that amendment of the Hungarian constitution, the longest-lasting in the region, was intended to promote the transition.) This liberal political system offered the clearest, most transparent contrast to the previous "socialist" set-up in the region, and made the systemic changes credible in the eyes of society and of the West.

To make this assumption clearer, it is necessary to add two qualifications about the assessments that were missing at the early years of the transition.

For a long time, criticisms and doubts have been appearing in Western literature on political science, about the efficiency with which the present form of representative democracy functions. These criticisms focus on several factors, but they can be conveyed most expressively by pointing to the widening gulf between citizens' participation in a formal, legal sense, and the effective scope for exerting influence, so that decision-making risks slip into the hands of an unidentifiable minority.[1] This is not a new finding, however. Stein Rokkan put it more strongly still over 20 years ago: "Votes count, resources decide."[2]

Rather than commenting on Rokkan's statement, I would like to confine the discussion to the profound research findings available concerning the operation of Western representative democracy.

The changes of the past few decades were assumed to have fundamentally modified the relationship between the state and its citizens, leading essentially to a challenge to representative democracy. The extent of the supposed components of the phenomenon was explored in an empirical survey conducted in 1989 in 18 Western and Southern European countries. The underlying issue was approached by studying 10 hypotheses through a questionnaire. Verification of these would confirm that citizens were forsaking representative democracy based on a multi-party system.[3] Although the hypotheses were justified or rejected by varying degrees in the European countries covered by the survey, certain general conclusions can be drawn.

The first hypothesis, that there would be a decrease in institutional participation in politics (which amounts in practice to elections), was not corroborated. Indeed a surprising consistency appeared between 1945 and 1989. (This is surprising because in some Western countries, electoral participation had been falling, as indicated by other data, as was confidence in political parties.)[4] On the other hand the second hypothesis was confirmed: citizens' activity in non-institutional forms of politics has clearly been increasing. The third hypothesis, the assumption that there had been a growth in political apathy, was not confirmed. Citizens' activities through non-institutionalized channels have had a significantly political content. The fourth hypothesis was that the links with various organizations representing special interests and with the trade unions had decreased. This did not pass the empirical test either. However, the alienation from political parties assumed in the fifth hypothesis could be clearly discerned. The sixth hypothesis suggested that citizens' interest in the new, collective political actors was increasing. This was not proved overall, although the findings differed from country to country. According to the seventh hypothesis, citizens were giving decreasing support to politicians. Although there was country variation again, the differences were small enough to allow a general statement of this nature to be made. The eighth hypothesis was that public support for governmental bodies (in the broad sense) was decreasing. Here the data confirmed this or at least presented a mixed picture. The same applies to the ninth hypothesis, which assumed that support for the democratic system was decreasing. In this case too, the data showed country variation, but no such general trend was warranted. On the other hand, the tenth hypothesis – that the significance attached to individual democratic values was growing – proved justified.

Some conclusions for Hungary can also be drawn from these findings.

- Generally speaking, Western European societies do not challenge the institution of representative democracy, or basically the role of competing parties, even if the "legitimacy" of the latter component, as the central mechanism of the political system, may have eroded as a result of change.
- However, it can be inferred that the society is no longer satisfied with periodic participation in politics (limited to elections).
- This phenomenon is related to the appearance of *individual* modernization, alongside modernization in a social dimension. Individuals who have attained a high level of modernity are mentally open, cognitively flexible, and creative, with a definite sense of individual efficacy. Such people are able to decide their own affairs and accept the rules of society.[5] People of this type can also identify their own interests in politics, select forms in which to assert them, and promote them by action in specific cases.
- Representative democracy offers relatively rare and limited political participation to the citizen. As a result the extremely strong role of the political parties in political processes is supplemented by only very weak citizens' participation.

To sum up, party representation, so far as we know, is an essential

145

component, but not a sufficient condition for the basic mechanism of representative democracy. Wider and more direct political participation needs to be guaranteed to citizens within the decision-making process of political parties and outside party politics. This process, styled "democratic transformation" by the heads of the research project, requires the more significant political actors to gain an enhanced ability to respond to citizens' demands. Meanwhile citizens are becoming far more active and hence *effective* in the political processes.[6]

A similar conclusion was reached by Edgar Grande, quoted earlier. He said that neither the classic forms of direct participation nor the modern forms of political representation are sufficient in themselves (even in the developing structure of the European Union). They should be evolved at several levels, and due to the inadequacy of individual control of political authority, institutional control should be placed at the focal point.[7]

Bearing in mind some global considerations, there is a further conclusion reached by the survey that has special importance for Hungary. The political legitimacy of Western democracy already depends strongly on government performance, and will do so increasingly in the future. With the transformation of the "socialist" systems and the end of ideological and military confrontation between West and East (a significant legitimizing factor for Western democracy), the public's attention is turning towards the functioning of democracy in each country, rather than its general principles. The level of satisfaction with democracy is related to the output of the economy, and its degree of support has turned from "ideal normative agreement" towards "instrumental acceptance" depending on economic and state efficiency.[8]

Naturally, Western European experiences can only be adapted to Hungarian conditions after analytical assessment, but lessons can definitely be drawn from the basic relationships. The first of the two main lessons – along with the need for changes in the representative system – is the public's demand for more direct participation in politics. (Here it is important to differentiate the levels of politics.) This requires a realistic assessment of the phenomena and components of political apathy. The second is the significant inclination towards the instrumental acceptance of democracy. The first lesson also touches upon the normative structure of the political system to which the second relates, but its interrelationships are too complex to be traced simply to economic output. On the whole, the Western phenomena serve as a warning. A political system built in keeping with traditional liberal notions, although it met the requirements of Hungarian society in the first few years of transition, as an ideal normative agreement, was already posing problems of the effectiveness of the state. So considerations of instrumental acceptance have already appeared as negative elements. Amendment of the constitution was based on a pact between the Hungarian Democratic Forum (MDF) and the Alliance of Free Democrats (SZDSZ).[9] It introduced the institution of a constructive motion of no confidence (only valid if an alternative government can be formed), which guaranteed a safe, strong position for the post-election government, and made other organizational changes. None the less, the *efficacy* of the state has decreased.

It is impractical to analyse the causes of these attitudes in this paper. However, it should be remembered that the phenomena dubbed the "real-chaos paradigm" by Samuel Huntington know no limits – global collapse of law and order, a global crime wave, strengthening transnational criminal organizations, spreading drug addiction, falling significance of the family, declining confidence and social solidarity, the spread of violence.[10] The handling of these problems, particularly under the conditions of transition, represents a challenge to which it is hardly possible for even a strong, confident state administration to respond adequately. The civil service has been weakened in skills and shaken in its self-confidence by various "purges." The uncertainties surrounding it lead to reliance on personal loyalties and organization into a clientele, which makes it more open to corruption. The need to wrestle with hitherto unknown assignments has placed it in a still more difficult situation. This situation and its consequences have so weakened public acceptance of the democratic political system by "normative agreement" that it may soon become impossible to base the consolidation of the democratic set-up on it.

However, the necessary institutional change is steadily becoming more difficult due to the "fundamentalism" of the political system based on liberal foundations. This initially proved successful, but has ultimately failed to allow for one of the main assets of liberal democracy: its immanent self-doubt and scepticism, which excludes a victorious complacency and is hence open, in theory, to change. This specificity has become blurred, so that the necessary structural changes cannot be engendered by the political system. (I shall later return to the second component, the changes in the characteristics of the political parties.)

One significant missing factor for normative creation of the political system remains a profound analysis of the development of Hungarian public law and the longer-term demands of Hungarian society. The possibilities for linkages between them have been more or less neglected.

The illusory objective of "eradicating the past" is frequently encountered in politics. It is also manifest in legislative activity and at times even among legal experts, particularly when carried along by major social changes. Such clean-slate illusions are tantamount to a disregard for historical processes – for social reality being shaped by history in a general sense. Warning of the futility of this was given almost 200 years ago by Friedrich Karl von Savigny, one of the giants of jurisprudence. Indeed the attempts to break the continuity of legal history by legislative means were not successful after either the American or the French revolutions, which both promoted change within the mainstream of history. (The civil code associated with the name of Napoleon was also based largely on processes and evolving social relations that had begun before the revolution, and partly on French customary law.) It was even less successful in the "blind alley of history" after the Russian revolution of 1917, and in societies on which "socialist" changes were imposed by Soviet occupation.

Historical continuity might also have become a difficult issue in legislation during the systemic change, if all the seemingly strong political forces had not been inclined to accept the classical liberal version of representative democracy, and the doctrine of the separation of the three branches of government. This means relatively little of the worth of Hungarian constitutional development featured in the new acts on public authority, although in some cases (e.g. Act XXXI of 1989, Article 2, Item 3, or certain stipulations of Chapter IX) it inspired the provisions of the Act amending the constitution. The method of electing the president of the Republic and to some extent definition of his legal position were based on Act I of 1946, since the early years of the post-war coalition period partly represented legal continuity with the emerging political system. (It was ignored that the country was under foreign occupation and indirect military rule in that period, so that its sovereignty was severely limited. The effect of these conditions on the birth of Act I of 1946 have yet to be properly clarified.)

The principles that tend to preserve the continuity of Hungarian constitutional development are essentially the same as those that promote its development by drawing on Western representative democracy and on present Hungarian practice. These are expansion of democratic participation, institutionalizing it in a "multi-channel" form, and making the dimensions of instrumental acceptance of democracy such that normative acceptance of it can become a major factor for consolidation.

So further development of the political system in a way that preserves historical continuity offers normative-institutional possibilities, and imposes conditions rooted in the increasing professionalism of the political actors (whether individuals or organizations) and in the political cultivation of those actors and of the population.

Of the possible institutional changes, I would emphasize first improving the system of representation. One question that experts in particular have repeatedly raised in recent years during the attempts to draw up a new constitution has been to restore of the traditional, bicameral form of the legislature. By the end of the debates, an almost complete professional consensus was reached about the structure of a second chamber, and variant compositions also evolved. The rejection always came from the political side, as political commonplaces (for instance, an incomprehensible and irresponsible association of ideas, referring to some kind of "popular-front nostalgia"), or of hollow arguments based on deliberate or unintentional misunderstanding of the expert arguments.

The second chamber, in my view, should not be based on the political parties. It should allow local and county authorities, public bodies and local minority authorities to participate in parliamentary decision-making. This would significantly reduce the "deficit" of democracy apparent in the system of parliamentary representation, by enhancing the potential for political participation. So its composition would be quite different from the earlier Upper House, which was originally similar to the UK House of Lords and later based on personal and institutional representation.

The second possibility is to strengthen local government, primarily the local and county authorities, by providing them with further chances to participate in local and national decision-making. There is little need to explain the significance and role of local government in the development of Hungarian public law and the policy of the country. There is appreciation these days of the role played by integral communities in modern society, although the dangers of overestimating this should not be forgotten either. The *Gesellschaft* type of development, related to modernization, produces or reinforces and lends a function to the *Gemeinschaft* type of formation.[11] However, the words of József Eötvös[12] should not be forgotten:

In view of the limitation of state authority ... one should also see to it that the individual does not stand alone before state authority [and therefore] some scope ... for autonomous activity should be given to the village, the province, and to organizations within the state generally.[13]

Eötvös was referring to the counties as well. I must stress in relation to them the often disputed fact that historically they developed three functions, which were expressly acknowledged in the late nineteenth-century legislation on municipalities (e.g. Act XLII of 1870 and Act XXI of 1886). These functions were to mediate central and local government, to act autonomously in its own affairs, and to perform a political function. The legislation acknowledged the right of counties to discuss political problems and inform other municipalities and the central government of the decisions they reached that had a political content. Central government since the end of the nineteenth century has attempted to curtail this autonomy and conduct public administration centrally in almost every piece of legislation. It has tried to prevent any participation in wider politics by local authorities, and to project the national party structure over local-government elections. This centralization of public administration and the related financial restrictions preclude any administrative function and autonomy for local government. The same is done to the political function by basing local and county elections on party politics.

While the strengthening of local governance embodies historical continuity in Hungarian public law, it does not protect tradition for its own sake. Modernization of the country is reaching its second phase. This changes the state's role in the process, but does not mean the state withdraws from it. The most important aspect of the change and of the difference between the two phases is a gradual alteration in direction, from top down to bottom up. The top-down direction still has to apply until the country's main supply and servicing systems have evolved and consolidated.

However, in the longer term the process of modernization will extend beyond the framework of the nation-state. It will become subject to the conditions of integration, and after accession, to the political, organizational, and legal framework of the EU. The changes of integration and the publicized policy of the Union offer great opportunities to development activities in a regional dimension. This largely coincides with the regional and local conditions and scope for Hungarian society, and the need to develop local potential in the public. So the traditions of Hungarian public law and modern demands coincide in the realization of local governance, while creating a new channel of participation for developing representative democracy.[14]

On the other hand there is another important conclusion to be drawn here. If the local authorities are given real weight in the political system, and create new forms of popular participation, then representation based on party politics cannot be tolerated at any level of local government. Interest relations also have several strata and identities that take shape along various "fault lines." So the political chance of expressing this variety would strengthen democracy and promote its consolidation.

In fact there has been decreasing party-political representation, since the 1990 local-government elections, in local authorities covering a population that enables them to develop a real local community. Similar trends can be seen in some larger cities with strong local traditions and allegiances. The elimination of the party-political nature of local-government elections may mean that local communities build up and embourgeoisement develops, while promoting various forms of popular participation. Setting out from this premise and the real interests inherent in county government, the direct election of county assemblies has to give way to delegation by the local authorities in the county. The local and county authorities created in this way will also be able to project politics of a different complexion from party politics, in the second chamber of parliament. This means that a politically independent, autonomous body of civil servants, based on professional knowledge, is an indispensable element of institutional change.

The chances of obtaining a democratic system based on normative values have been reduced, but not eliminated in recent years, although illusions about such a system's potential for providing immediate prosperity have been lost. Nowadays, much of society has upgraded economic factors, and along with them, security of life and livelihood as basic values. So there has been a shift towards acceptance or rejection of an instrumental assessment of democracy, and the significance of being indifferent to this has increased.

The 1994 elections already clearly indicated the spread of an instrumental assessment of democracy. The change in voting patterns was influenced not only by the deterioration in the economic situation, but by the fact that the economic components of political life had been weakened. Another factor behind the change in voting patterns was the challenge and questioning of the almost ubiquitous social dimensions of the normative agreement prevalent in political life at the time. After the 1994 elections, the instrumental attitude strengthened almost naturally amidst the negative effects of further building of the market economy. Remaining on the institutional level of the political system, it can be said that the organizations which might have mitigated the spread of instrumental acceptance and blended instrumental assessment with elements of a normative acceptance of democracy were insufficiently developed or not functioning properly. Actually, public acceptance of economic difficulties and restrictive measures can be much better if requisite interest-protecting and interest-adjusting organizations exist and operate along clear-cut lines, based only on legal regulation of them.

Profound analyses would presumably help to determine why the governments of the 1990s have not developed an efficient organization for interest adjustment, why they have not come up with clear concepts in this field, and why the organizations participating in interest adjustment have not been able to function efficiently. One factor is the interweaving of special-interest representation with political affiliation, already manifest in the strong political affiliations of the various trade unions. Dividing the representation of economic and social interests along political, even party-political lines, obviously rules out practical interest adjustment, especially if the minimum level of loyalty required to make the democratic set-up workable is lacking from the formalized or non-formalized political forces.[15] Nowadays it has become even clearer when the activity of interest representation has taken to the streets. The infusion of the political element in these demonstrations, or organization of them around the political element, often makes them dysfunctional. They elicit social divisions instead of solidarity, and ultimately hinder the assertion of demands (the rightfulness of which may be disputed by comparison with other strata) to a greater or lesser degree.

Since 1989, the political forces in the country have yet to arrive at an agreement to ensure that at least a few of the main problems are resolved by consensus, which would also expose the economic and social issues of the transition. This failure relates to the fact that solving even the most important national issues of livelihood have been relegated behind party-political considerations. Processes of this nature have developed based on such decisions, and are already irreversible in many respects. However, it may not be too late to combat the consequences of this practice by setting up an organization vested with real authority (such as the French Economic and Social

Council). This could develop agreements that spanned government terms, after discussion of economic and social questions within a longer period, free from party-political obligations, rather than as single, hastily proposed, ill-considered decisions.

It depends on the behaviour of political forces, organizations, and individuals running the political system and on changes in their political cultivation – i.e. answers to the second question raised initially – what chances arise for institutional changes that approximate the normative framework of the political system to Hungarian society, as shaped by global change and its own development. The doubts and mistrust in the political system and politics as a whole relate to the élite's inability to direct further development of its own system or deal with economic and social conflicts in an effective, democratic way. This inability results from a combination of several factors.

The first factor, which may sound surprising, is a necessary dysfunctional consequence of the development of a main element of the Hungarian democratic political system, the multi-party system. The explanation is simple. The contrast between the one-party nature of the "socialist" political system and the existence of several parties was an important change, which upgraded the political parties as symbols of change. This re-evaluation took place under conditions in which the élite intelligentsia, as the kernel of the parties, was brought together by abstract principles, often by chance. Political experience was largely lacking, and because this stratum's values and behaviour patterns are primarily those of the arts-oriented intelligentsia, its members are only transformed with difficulty and at great length into professional politicians.[16] So even though other factors were also instrumental, the re-evaluation that had taken place at an earlier phase of the transformation changed into self-evaluation.[17] The outlook and behaviour of the ruling party under the one-party system were projected on to the new parties, so that articulation of political problems and interests was possible only through parties, and within parties by specific groups of factions. This could be observed in parliamentary legislation, particularly in the debates on the constitution, which has not changed significantly despite the disputes and criticisms. The accords reached on constitutional issues expressed the lowest common denominator of the political parties, carefully excluding rational recommendations from experts or political groups outside the party system.

This exclusive behaviour by the political parties, asserted through parliament, was a reminder of István Bibó's earlier concern: "Even an organ of popular representation may become the focus of the concentration of power,"[18] whereas the concentration of power questions the reality of popular representation. It is also a reminder that Item 2 of Article 3 of Hungary's current constitution states for good reason that "the parties *participate* in the development and manifestation of the popular will" (my emphasis). This is supplemented by the likewise significant wording of Item 2 of Article 20, which approaches the problem from another angle: "The Members of Parliament undertake their activities in the public interest." Actually this provision expressly makes the activities of MPs independent of their party interests. This is interesting because in theory it was an openness that fed on someone's doubts about the political system built on liberal principles, to some aspects of which I return later. It also raises doubts about the ruling of the Constitutional Court concerning the procedural order of constitution-making.

It is a characteristic contradiction in the Hungarian political system that according to recent opinion polls, over 50 per cent of the electorate has yet to select a political party to support. This reflects far greater doubt about the representative system based on political parties than can be inferred from the survey findings in Western countries. Of course the findings of this poll may be strongly linked to the situation characteristic today, and not indicate a trend valid for a longer period, but even then it cannot be disregarded.

The second factor is that coordination of the conditions and consequences of democracy and of the market economy is difficult even in developed countries. Experience and a recent book by the American scholar Lester Thurow show that the task is particularly problematic in the CEE transition countries. Continual attempts to solve this difficult task should be governed everywhere by vision and by images of the future that can be applied in practice, even if they have ideological foundations. What can the multi-party system be used for? Thurow asked (and here he does not see any difference between the old and the new democracies) whether the political parties do not possess visions that help to solve the problems of the present and the future. If these are missing, he continues, democracy becomes competition between friends and enemies, between candidates making promises, or even a tribal practice, in which a tribe made responsible for the problems of the country is chosen and then punished.[19]

There are several sources of the mistrust and aversion to politics apparent in Hungary today. The behaviour of parties, inside and outside parliament, is just a superficial phenomenon. The mutual recriminations are of secondary significance, as are the animosities substituted for rational dispute and the blatant struggles for power that relegate the country's interests to the background. One of the underlying problems is that most parties do not have realistic ideas or offer attractive alternatives for coping with the main social or economic problems. Another source of mistrust is that their policies and practices often fail to correspond with professed ideas such as tolerance or social solidarity, which have gained respect, for example, for modern Christian democrats or social democrats in the West. The lack of civic behaviour and political professionalism also causes conspicuous problems and undermines confidence in the operation of democratic institutions. This entails a risk of overt or covert autocratic rule.

Let there be no misunderstanding: representative democracy cannot work without parties. However, the transition cannot be completed or consolidation succeed if the country's political forces cannot work together, coherently and constructively, on issues vital to the success of the changes and the shape of the future. There are some especially significant issues for which a national policy consensus is required.

It must be accepted that the economy cannot stand another upheaval in ownership relations. Mistakes and even crimes were committed in the process of privatization and compensation of earlier victims, but a realistic economic solution has to be found to correct them. A political move that might result in a new redistribution of wealth, towards the clients of the parties that came to power by political rotation, would be an economic disaster. It would undermine confidence in the Hungarian economic system abroad and destabilize domestic business. Another important issue relates to tolerable limits to income differentiation. This cannot be left to policies based on social demagogy. The main question is how to ease or eliminate poverty, while accepting the differentiation necessary for an efficient market system. A further problem relates to the legal system. Social peace and predictable livelihoods cannot be obtained without a stable legal system based on the country's constitutional system, or without law enforcement and a judicial system to apply it (except for a narrow stratum of society, at high cost). In some parts of the United States in 1970, twice as much was spent on the police than on private security and protection services. In 1990 the proportions were reversed.[20] No matter how far the developed West can serve as an example elsewhere, it cannot do so in this respect. However, legal and public security are functions of social peace, and cannot be attained amidst the incitement of hatred and political threats. It can hardly be denied that not even a minimum of political consensus can be expected without social peace. Finally, united national efforts are needed to elaborate a long-term, conceptually developed model of education and the other major redistributive systems, for gradual implementation.

I do not want to discuss the merits and shortcomings of consensus politics or the differentiation between democracies based on majority rule and those based on consensus. However, there are certain historical situations in which consensus is almost forcibly imposed even on democracies based strictly on the majority principle. A well-known example was the consensus reached among the political parties in Britain, during the decades after the Second World War. That had two basic components. One was agreement between the two main parties on the style of governance: constant consultations with social groups in key positions, notably the trade unions, and some generally agreed policy outlines. Areas of policy agreement included broadly Keynesian fiscal policies and the Beveridge concept of a welfare state. This consensus marked the governance of successive Conservative and Labour administrations until these policies became dysfunctional, and began to create more problems than they solved.[21] Margaret Thatcher had good reason to turn against these policies in 1981, even though her blanket criticism of consensus-based policy was unjustified.

Naturally, there is a great deal of truth in the idea that confrontation is the lifeblood of politics, and the idea of consensus runs against the practice of political competition.[22] There is also truth in the following: "In a fundamental sense, there must always be a good deal of common ground between the main parties alternating in government in a free society. When in power, after all, they are governing the same country, with the same history, people, problems and elbow-room, or, lack of it, within the same world."[23] A similarity in the solutions found to problems by parties – unless their bases for doing so are distorted into ideology, in other words, so long as their handling of them is gradual – produces a remarkable continuity, even without a formal consensus.[24]

So the quarter-century of British politics that followed the Second World War (or Canadian consensus politics in the same period) confirms that there are situations that demand a consensus approach. This does not destroy democracy. Once it becomes dysfunctional, a change has to come and a new set of conditions emerges, which may produce a further consensus, tacit or overt, in due course.

Hungary today is in a situation where a consensus is needed, at least on solving the problems listed earlier. Answers have to be found to other major questions as well, such as the quantitative and qualitative decline in the population, the moral crisis, and ways of safeguarding and strengthening national cultural identity after gaining EU membership. It can only be hoped that it will be easier to reach a consensus on the major issues than it has been on lesser ones, where the political parties have a disappointing record.

Fernand Braudel sees history on three planes. The first is almost motionless. With man and his relationship to the environment, it is "a history in which all change is slow, a history of constant repetition, ever-recurring cycles ... On a different level from the first, there can be distinguished another history, this time with slow but perceptible rhythms ... the history of groups and groupings." The second could be called social history, he adds. Finally there is conventional history, "the history of events: surface disturbances, crests of foam that the tides of history carry on their strong backs. A history of brief, rapid, nervous fluctuations ..." Braudel then touches on the essential problem:

Is it possible somehow to convey simultaneously both that conspicuous history which holds our attention by its continual and dramatic changes – and that other, submerged, history, almost silent and always discreet, virtually unsuspected either by its observers or its participants, which is little touched by the obstinate erosion of time?[25]

This approach to history is important also for practical understanding and scientific analysis of the scope and limitations of political activity and politics.

To apply this to the specific topic of this paper, society in the short run expects *commitment* from its political system, and this is the essence of liberal democracy. Authority is possessed by those who govern, but only for a limited time. However, there is more than this involved in the relationship between society and the political system. It also requires medium-term predictability. Hence government has to create stable conditions in which economic and social life can flourish. Finally, politics has to evolve a long-term *vision* of the trends of social development. It has to consider well in advance the consequences of technological development, the ecological dangers, and the expected political changes. Some maintain that the three branches of power are responsible for three time-spans: the executive is responsible for short-term management during the term of government, the judiciary for medium-term tasks, and legislation for long-term objectives. A similar division of labour between the political parties and special-interest groups is also posited,[26] but I do not see any possibility of "accrediting" such a division of labour. All the components of the political system – government, parties, and special-interest organizations – need to think and act responsibly in all three frames. Short-term decisions (the length of a governmental term of office in this case) can significantly influence medium-term prospects, and it is not clear how they will ultimately affect long-term perspectives, the processes that ultimately guide the branching alternatives back into the mainstream. It is identification of this, and successful efforts at short and medium-term activities to attain it, that elevate statesmen above other politicians. To return to Braudel, "The true man of action is he who can measure most nearly the constraints upon him, who chooses to remain within them and even to take advantage of the weight of the inevitable, exerting his own pressure in the same direction."[27]

That allows an answer to be given to the question raised at the beginning of this paper, even if only on a basis of propositions. Having developed normatively in the first years of the transition, *the Hungarian political system certainly needs change*. However, the prevailing institutional system cannot be blamed for the problems. Its operation has proved difficult because of the often contradictory tasks of a dual transformation (concurrently developing a market economy and a smoothly functioning democratic political system). Also a problem is the often irrational and counter-productive behaviour of the main political actors and the slow acquisition of professionalism by the new political elite. Without changes in these aspects, even the best institutions will be distorted and there will be no improvement in the political cultivation of society.

Conclusion

In an earlier work of mine[28] I quote from Thomas Jefferson's inaugural speech on 4 March 1801 what I still see as a timely admonition for the Hungarian political system:

Let us restore harmony and good intentions in social contact, without which freedom and life itself is bleak. Let us ponder over that. Even if we ban religious intolerance from our country, which has been the cause of so much bloodshed and suffering of humanity, we gain even less if we close our eyes and do not see political intolerance, which is capable of equally tyrannous, cruel and bloody persecutions.

Notes

1. Grande (1996), p. 339.
2. Rokkan (1975).
3. On the research and its findings, see Klingemann and Fuchs (1995).
4. See Dubiel (1996), pp. 128–129.
5. See Inkeles and Smith (1974), p. 190 ff. and Inkeles (1983), p. 12 ff.
6. Klingemann and Fuchs (1995), pp. 420–438.
7. Grande (1996), p. 357.
8. Klingemann and Fuchs (1995), pp. 438–442.
9. These two parties played a crucial role as opponents of the socialist-etatist regime and in shaping the institutional framework for change during the early part of the transition. The MDF became the strongest political party after the first democratic elections in 1990. The SZDSZ remained in opposition, but entered government in coalition with the Socialist Party after the 1994 elections.
10. Huntington (1996), p. 321.
11. See Wallerstein (1986) and Huntington (1996), pp. 76 and 93.
12. The basically liberal ideas of József Eötvös, the nineteenth-century Hungarian political thinker, had a defining influence on some leading figures in the recent democratization. One of his ideological disciples was József Antal, the prime minister who formed the first democratically elected government in 1990.
13. Eötvös (1981), Vol. II, pp. 344–345.
14. On these problems, see Kulcsár (1996b), pp. 14–21.
15. Kissinger (1995), p. 311.
16. On this, see Kulcsár (1995b), pp. 34–45.
17. Fritz (1994), p. 89.
18. Bibó (1986), Vol. II, p. 393. István Bibó, one of the seminal democratic political thinkers in twentieth-century Hungary, helped to build the short-lived democratic system after 1945. He was also a member of Imre Nagy's government during the 1956 revolution, after which he was imprisoned for several years.
19. Thurow (1996), p. 225.
20. Thurow (1996), pp. 264–265.
21. Pearce and Stewart (1992), pp. 458–462.
22. Kavanagh and Morris (1989), p. 10.
23. Hennessy and Sheldon (1989), p. 310.
24. Pearce and Stewart (1992), pp. 510–511.
25. Braudel (1976), Vol. I, pp. 16 and 20–21.
26. Gerlich (1996), pp. 62–63.
27. Braudel (1976), Vol. II, pp. 1243–1244.
28. Kulcsár (1994).

References

Bibó, István (1986), *Válogatott tanulmányok* (Selected Studies), 3 vols, Budapest: Magveto Kiadó.

Braudel, Fernand (1976), *The Mediterranean and the Mediterranean World in the Age of Philip II*, 2 vols, New York and Cambridge: Harper and Row.

Dubiel, H. (1996), "Die Krise der liberalen Demokratie," in P. Gerlich, K. Glass, and B. Serloth (eds.), *Mitteleuropäische Mythen und Wirklichkeiten*, Wien-Torun: Österreichische Gesellschaft für Mitteleuropäische Studien Verlag.

Eötvös, József (1981) [1851–1854], *A XIX. század uralkodó eszméinek befolyása az államra* (The Influence on the State of the 19th Century's Dominant Ideas), 2 vols, Budapest: Magyar Helikon.

Fricz, T. (1994), "A magyar parlamenti pártrendszer jellemzése és tipizálása" (The Characterization and Typology of the Hungarian System of Parliamentary Parties), in *Törésvonalak és értékválasztások* (Fault Lines and Value Choices), Budapest: MTA Politikatudományi Intézet (Hungarian Academy of Sciences, Institute of Political Science, MTA PTI).

Gerlich, P. (1996), "Democracy and Time," in Gerlich, Glass, and Serloth (1996).

Grande, E. (1996), "Demokratische Legitimation und europäische Integration", *Leviathan*, Vol. 24.

Hennessey, P., and A. Seldon, eds. (1989), *Ruling Performance. British Governments from Attlee to Thatcher*, Oxford: Blackwell.

Huntington, S.P. (1996), *The Clash of Civilizations and the Remaking of World Order*, New York: Simon and Schuster.

Inkeles, A. (1983), *Exploring Individual Modernity*, New York: Columbia University Press.

Inkeles, A., and D.H. Smith (1974), *Becoming Modern: Individual Change in Six Developing Countries*, Cambridge, Mass.: Harvard University Press.

Kavanagh, D., and P. Morris (1989), *Consensus Politics from Attlee to Thatcher*, Oxford: Blackwell.

Kissinger, Henry (1995), *Diplomacy*, London: Simon and Schuster.

Klingemann, H-D., and D. Fuchs, eds. (1995): *Citizens and the State*, Oxford: Oxford University Press.

Kulcsár, Kálmán (1994), *Kontinuitás és átmenet. Töprengések az utóbbi évek magyar politikai gyakorlatáról* (Continuity and Transition. Meditations on the Hungarian Political Practice of Recent Years), Szombathely: Savaria.

Kulcsár, Kálmán (1995a), "A magyar modernizáció politikai összefüggései" (The Political Connections of Hungarian Modernization), *Valóság*, Vol. XXXVIII, No. 11.

Kulcsár, Kálmán (1995b), "A magyar értelmiség politikai szerepvállalása" (The Political Role Assumed by the Hungarian Intelligentsia), *Tiszatáj*, Vol. 49, No. 9.

Kulcsár, Kálmán (1996a), "A jog és a modernizáció Magyarországon" (Law and Modernization in Hungary), *Társadalomkutatás*, Nos. 3–4.

Kulcsár, Kálmán (1996b), "A közigazgatás és a társadalom" (Public Administration and Society), *Comitatus*, Vol. VI, No. 12.

Kulcsár, Kálmán (1997a), *Systemwechsel in Ungarn, 1988–1990*, Frankfurt am Main: Vittorio Klostermann.

Kulcsár, Kálmán (1997b), "A politikai reprezentáció és a kétkamarás Országgyűlés" (Political Representation and a Bicameral Parliament), in I. Stumpf (ed.), *Félidőben* (Mid-term), Budapest: MTA PTI.

Pearce, M., and G. Stewart (1992), *British Political History*, London and New York: Routledge.

Przeworski, A. (1991), *Democracy and the Market: Political and Economic Reforms in Eastern Europe and Latin America*, Cambridge: Cambridge University Press.

Rokkan, Stein (1975), "Votes Count, Resources Decide," in *Magt og Motiv*, Oslo: Oslo University.

Rotte, R. (1996), "Die Reideologiesierung der Politik und die Position der westlichen Demokratien," *Politik und Gesellschaft*, No. 2.

Serloth, B. (1996), "Der Mythos der liberalen Demokratie: Zwischen Individuum und Gemeinschaft," in Gerlich, Glass, and Serloth (1996).

Thurow, L.C. (1996), *The Future of Capitalism*, London: Nicholas Brealey Publishing.

Wallerstein, I. (1986), "Societal Development or Development of the World System?" *International Sociology*, Vol. I, No. 1.

9

The political economy of democratization in the Polish transition

Janusz Golebiowski

Development trends and economic policy

Poland is nearing the end of the first stage of transition, having laid the groundwork for the new system and carried out the fundamental reforms by the "shock-treatment" methods prescribed in the Balcerowicz Plan. It is over its most difficult period, when GDP plunged, incomes shrank drastically, unemployment soared and the social stratification changed. The height of these socially painful processes of adjustment came in 1991–1992. In 1993, slow but steady GDP growth began. A year later, unemployment began to fall, and by 1996 and 1997, real wages and incomes were rising again.

Headway has been made in modernization processes, first in the infrastructure (communications, computerization, banking) and then in production. Changes in the ownership structure continue, quite quickly on the whole. Even in traditional heavy industry, where they have been slowest and met with most obstacles, there has been notable progress thanks to the opening of a number of privatization tracks. Also to be seen is a shift towards concentration of ownership of agricultural land, which is creating larger, more modern and efficient family farms. These transformation processes are not yet complete. Over half the biggest industrial units, including the whole mining and energy sector, some of the engineering industry, and such economic giants as telecommunications and transport, remain state-owned and controlled, with only slightly modified structures. Modernization processes have so far affected only 30–40 per cent of farms. Notwithstanding, domestic and foreign observers agree that Poland is recovering from its crisis successfully and rapidly, that it has managed to reverse its unfavourable economic trends and acquire an advanced new ownership and social structure. Another factor that makes the prospects look optimistic is that the ownership and market reforms have gained the economy a considerable degree of independence from politics.

This does not mean that the main problems of the transition process or of economic and cultural modernization belong to the past. That is far from the case, especially in terms of popular perceptions and acceptance of the new system. The difficulties there are greater than in the economy itself: attitudes, as it were, have lagged behind progress with economic reform.

Changes in social structure

The changes in Poland's social structure brought by the last seven years have been considerable, though in some ways unexpected. It was assumed that the switch to a market economy would help to engender a large middle class, with members with a stake in a free-enterprise system they would be ready to defend, as a base for centrist and liberal parties. The middle class has certainly grown fast. There are now well over 2 million owners of non-agricultural businesses (6–7 million if participant family members are included.) The private sector currently accounts for 60 per cent of GNP and employs over 60 per cent of the national labour force. The attitudes and behaviour displayed by the middle class are primarily determined by its internal structure. Many of the new self-employed were forced into small-scale business, by the threat of redundancy. They possess next to no capital and they are short of business skills and experience. A high proportion thrives in the grey economy, evading taxes, engaging in smuggling, and often cheating whenever they can. Much of this new middle class has more in common with a Middle Eastern bazaar than with the Western European market. Of course a gradual civilizing, stabilizing process will ensue, so that the middle class eventually develops a sense of its own distinct interests and ethos. Some moves in this direction have been shown by sociological studies. One sign has been the formation of voluntary small-business organizations that take an active part in negotiations with the government, the trade unions, and the consumer organizations. The young managers, economists, financiers, engineers, and others who form the backbone of these organizations declare unqualified support for a policy of further reforms.

Emergence of a middle class, under present Polish conditions, is as natural as the diminution of the intelligentsia. The former is a product and mainstay of the free market and capitalism. The latter derives from the abnormal conditions under which Poles had to live for almost a century and a half. The middle class is being recruited from members of the old intelligentsia who abandon their class as it undergoes pauperization and loss of status, and from potential members of it – college graduates – who decide against joining it at all.

Recent surveys of self-employed professionals have shown that this social group integrally combines the ethics of the middle class and that of the intelligentsia. Its members possess a strong, internalized sense of the value of work. They head their list of desirable personal characteristics, on the one hand with drive and initiative, professional skills, discipline, mental resilience, and enterprise, and on the other with education, civility, and openness to others.

So as the middle class emerges, there also emerges a new system of values, typical of the class. The productivity index indicates that the activity and mentality models typical of the middle class are steadily taking root in the whole of Polish society.

One class that continues to have considerable significance in Poland is the peasantry. Farmers, most of them smallholders, still account for 25 per cent of the population. They are the only example in the region of a large class of private owners surviving the socialist period and preserving their sense of distinct identity. Poland's farmers were quick to organize politically, and their party occupies a key position in the government. However, the attitude of the class to transition is ambivalent. Its economic situation and traditions place it within the free-market system, but its short-term interests and advantages impel it to resist neo-liberal economic policies. There is wide support in the farming community for things like government intervention, protectionist tariff barriers, food-price supports (guaranteed prices for farm produce), and cheap, subsidized credits. Poland's biggest class of private owners stands firmly behind many of the arrangements and institutions of the command economy. This is not quite so baffling as it might seem. Although the command economy did not eliminate peasant farming, it halted its free-market evolution. Above all, it arrested the process of land concentration, so prolonging the life of small, less efficient farms. While subordinating farmers to the state and making them dependent on government contracts, subsidies, allocations, and the like, the command economy also gave them a sense of security. It eliminated competition between them and curbed the stratification among them. That resulted in a strong sense of peasant solidarity, so that even the owners of large, modern farms think in terms of common class interest: they are still peasants rather than capitalists. Although changes in this mentality can be discerned, they remain slow, because Polish agriculture is backward, technically and economically, and incapable of withstanding competition from Western European farming. So the immediate interests of Polish farmers make them hostile to an open economy. Such a narrowly class-oriented, self-centred posture is effectively at variance with the interests of other major social groups, especially urban workers. It is a Polish peculiarity.

The working class – or more broadly, urban employees – has split in two. Its more active, enterprising, and on the whole more highly skilled members have moved into private-sector employment. There they can earn more, albeit at the expense of some loss of welfare provisions. About a half of the blue and white-collar workers remain employed in the state sector of industry, which is plagued by considerable financial problems. Pay there is lower and the future uncertain, but the range of welfare benefits remains wide, although shrinking. However, the sheer size of this workforce gives it a sense of power and the leverage to exert effective pressure, which has significantly affected the way the trade unions' policies have evolved. While Solidarity steers towards right-wing populism, its rival on the left, the National Alliance of Trade Unions, moves towards old-style communist attitudes. In general, the prevailing mood among industrial workers is one of frustration and disillusionment. For they were once the cutting edge of anti-communist opposition, also wooed and cajoled by the communist party, and so receiving testimonials of their pre-eminence in society from both sides.

A recent survey of the situation and perceptions of workers over the 1990–1997 period has shown that a majority of them did not perceive their circumstances as worse than in the past. An opinion frequently encountered was that more could be bought for an average wage under communism than at present, albeit at the cost of lengthy queuing. Many workers, especially women, expressed a preference for the egalitarianism of queuing over the greater inequalities of today. However, only 20–30 per cent of respondents described their circumstances as bad or very bad. A smaller percentage said they were doing well, and the majority (50–60 per cent) rated their standard of living as average. The main grievances cited by workers were fear of losing their jobs and housing shortages. However, they were also troubled by a sense of social decline. A high proportion deplored the rise of an inequitable capitalism, whose winners earn by their wits, and objected to the fact that some beneficiaries of the socialist system had become beneficiaries of the market economy as well. Privatization has raised the question of the future of employee participation, which has been a crucial element of industrial relations in Poland.

Most of the workers polled felt no nostalgia for the past or desire to return to an etatist economy. However, there was a strong ambivalence evident in their thinking. On the one hand they expressed the view that a free-market system required thorough-going privatization, while on the other they perceived state-owned enterprises as more friendly, and would prefer to be employed in them. So notwithstanding a declared acceptance of the general direction of transition, workers in state-owned enterprises were afraid of privatization, seeing it as threatening a deterioration in their working conditions, and above all, cuts in employment. This application of dissonant criteria to macro and micro-economic phenomena became stronger, not weaker, over the 1990–1997 period. Acceptance and acknowledgement that privatization brings benefits to the economy and to firms was not matched by equally strong support for the government withdrawing from the ownership of economic entities. Most respondents in national opinion polls, many employees in privatized enterprises, and most representatives of the business and social élites favour retaining plants in the "strategic" sectors in public ownership. Respondents associate maintaining state-enterprise status with retaining government control and guaranteeing economic empowerment. These tendencies are more likely to be strengthened than weakened by the prospect of integration into the EU.

People clearly expect the state to ease the painful social consequences of reform, such as unemployment and mounting impoverishment. This is apparent in a preference for stronger government control over the transition processes and over the restructuring and operation of firms. There is decided disapproval of "unbridled" capitalism, of lack of control over the private sector, and of ineffective measures against white-collar crime. This tends to weaken support for economic reforms and generate a sense of destabilization and insecurity. It is also related to the moral condemnation of privatization expressed by many respondents in opinion polls.

Of course the support for privatization and assessment of its results are differentiated. Two groupings with different levels of acceptance of privatization can be discerned. Its supporters tend to be persons with at least a secondary education, who are managerial employees, owners of businesses, or professionals. Attitudes here are also strongly differentiated by age. Young people are firmly in favour of privatization, while their elders are more critical. Groups with secondary and higher education go beyond expressing more positive attitudes to ownership changes and clearly stress their benefits.

The dynamics of the attitudes to privatization rest on firm foundations, but the strongest support goes to a vision of a "friendly" market economy. This involves internalization in the social consciousness of general free-market principles and acceptance of the basic rules of government intervention designed to provide some insurance against risk. Nevertheless, it is also apparent from the study described here that only a minority of workers favour more radical militancy and oppose reform and transition altogether. What predominates is reconcilement with the realities, albeit a grudging and anxious one.

The greatest degree of appreciation for market reforms and democratic change is exhibited by the intelligentsia, even though many of them, employed in the government sector, have suffered heavily by the transition process. Their education gives them a better understanding of economic mechanisms. Market equilibrium (absence of queuing) is something especially prized, and by the nature of things, this is the class that sets most store by political democracy and the rule of law.

Cultural factors in the transition process

Poland before the change of system, like other countries of the region if to a lesser degree, remained outside the orbit of the contemporary mass culture that flourished in the West. Here the transition brought a veritable revolution. The Polish market was flooded with all the manifestations and products of mass culture: pop music, discos, crime fiction, horror movies and novels, youth fashions, and so on. All these were greeted enthusiastically by the young, but have aroused mixed feelings and often alarm in the older generation, for various reasons. To some extent it is simply a conservatism rooted in the habits of the socialist period and in religious tradition. However, there are some objective grounds for concern about these cultural changes, with the appearance of phenomena hitherto unknown or at most marginal in the region.

The most obvious of these is drug abuse. Traditionally, there were only two kinds of addictive substance in widespread use: alcohol and tobacco. Alcoholism in Poland has reached disturbingly large proportions and tobacco consumption remains far higher than in the West. Of late, Poland has become a convenient transit route for drugs moving from Asia to Europe. These are now generally available in Poland itself. Inadequate legislation and the absence of any tradition of effective countermeasures have contributed to the appearance and rapid spread of drug abuse. Public alarm over this feeds conservative inclinations to attribute the disease to the expansion of mass culture and excessive opening of Polish society to Western influences.

Again like other countries in the region, Poland has experienced an increase in crime and the appearance of new criminal activities – organized and Mafia-type crime – and a consequent decline in the public sense of security. Armed robbery, homicide, extortion, and large-scale fraud are all increasing, as a product of the market economy on the one hand, and the dismantling of the police state on the other.

One cultural feature of society's reaction to these pathological phenomena is a certain primitivism, evinced primarily in calls for harsher punishments as the main remedy, while the significance of education is not given its due. This ties in with a traditional brutalizing of social and personal relations in Poland and much of the region, deriving in part from earlier arrears in civilization. Only a few decades ago, for instance, illiteracy was still widespread. Another factor that has played an important part in this has been mass migration between regions (ethnic interchange) and flows of people from the country to the town. This has caused large groups to lose their moral bearings once they are beyond the strict community and family control to which they have been accustomed for centuries. It will be a long time before new bonds and rules come to replace the old. These structural processes have been compounded by the passing, but nevertheless acute, stresses and tensions of the transition process, with loss of social security and a sense of uncertainty about the future.

Despite these background difficulties, there are relatively strong and dynamic processes of adaptation to the new conditions taking place, with losses in one area being compensated by gains in another.

Some cultural fields are undergoing a vibrant expansion, while others like painting, theatre, and cinema, once generously supported by the state, are in decline.

Political change and the dilemmas of democratization

Poland's political system has been thoroughly transformed along democratic lines during the seven years of transition. There was an early stampede to form parties, resulting in some 200 political organizations being registered. About 20 of these still have some significance. Many smaller parties managed to enter the next parliament as bloc members. Solidarity Electoral Action, for instance, is a coalition of 49 political entities, although no more than two or three parties are likely to emerge in the end. The media express a range of positions, but few parties have newspapers of their own, and most have low circulations. Typically, daily papers profess independence, even if they are identified with a particular party. The biggest daily, *Gazeta Wyborcza*, supports the Union of Freedom.

Five free national elections have been held so far, three parliamentary and two presidential. All observers agreed they were fair. Against expectations, the turn-outs were only low or average (50–60 per cent). All restrictions on civil liberties such as freedom of speech, association, demonstration, and movement have been abolished. Trade unions operate freely, with two national organizations predominant: Solidarity and the National Alliance of Trade Unions. All Poles are entitled to a passport and able to travel in Europe without a visa.

The judiciary has undergone major structural reforms. The judges were screened and a small proportion, implicated in miscarriages of justice and complicity in political persecution, were removed from the bench. A system of appeal courts has been established and the institution of judicial review has been restored. Judicial independence has been buttressed by the principle that judges may not be dismissed. Poland is now a country under the rule of law, although crime rates are rising and society's level of legal compliance remains low. A new penal code came into force on 1 January 1998. Civil and commercial law has been amended and modernized.

One refractory problem for the democratization process has been reform of the security, intelligence, and counter-intelligence services. These were heavily involved in political intrigue under the communist system. Despite screening of personnel and numerous reorganizations, they have had trouble submitting to the rules of a democratic state. Two years ago, they again became parties to a political intrigue, assembling charges of spying against the then prime minister, using procedures that a parliamentary commission of inquiry found to be against the law. The upshot was a reorganization of the police services. Intelligence and counter-intelligence have been detached from the Interior Ministry and made responsible to the head of government.

A notable reform has been to establish civilian control over the armed forces. Two years ago, after some difficulties and resistance from the high command, direction of the Defence Department passed to a true civilian. (His predecessors had been seconded or retired generals.) The relationship between the public authorities and the military no longer arouses reservations among NATO experts.

From an institutional point of view, there has been a democratic breakthrough, but democratization is far from complete and threats to democracy loom large. This is due partly to a paucity of democratic traditions and customs. Poland, historically, lacks experience of modern democratic statehood. The "gentry-democracy" for which it was celebrated in the fifteenth to eighteenth centuries was limited to a single class, and in any case degenerated rapidly into an anarchic oligarchy. After the partitions, the country's main regions came under the rule of the Romanov Tsars, which was a relic of absolutism by the mid-nineteenth century. The independence restored in 1918 began with a none-too-successful, short-lived experiment with parliamentary democracy, ended by a military coup by Józef Pilsudski, who introduced a mild dictatorship. After the war came 45 years of dictatorial, single-party, and for a period totalitarian rule by the communist party. A strong legacy of this whole experience is a tendency to see politics in terms of warfare, of unrelenting confrontation with opponents, while freedom is associated with anarchy. Although the pivotal moment in the change of system was the "grand compromise" at the 1989 Round Table, this did not perpetuate a belief in compromise as a civilized way of resolving political conflicts and rivalries. Before long, the tradition of the Round Table was being questioned within Solidarity itself – by the winning side in the change of system. The "war at the top" proclaimed by Lech Walesa in 1990 produced a split in Solidarity's ranks. A minority, institutionally represented by the Union of Freedom and personally by Tadeusz Mazowiecki, remained committed to democracy and the rule of law. The majority, behind their charismatic leader, voiced leanings towards ill-defined methods of "revolutionary acceleration" and semi-authoritarian forms of government. The atmosphere at home, and above all internationally, was not conducive to realizing such aspirations, which suffered defeat and contributed to the Solidarity camp's loss of power in the 1993 elections. However, the consequences were weighty, in the institutional sphere and on social consciousness.

The institutional sphere of democracy

Poland only managed to produce a new constitution seven years after the end of communist-party dictatorship. Until then, the 1952 Stalinist constitution had remained in force, albeit with several substantial amendments. The cause of the delay, apart from reasons that will be discussed later, was a running debate over what kind of institutional model of democratic government should be chosen. Political scientists and political élites, and succeeding parliaments, failed to decide between presidential government on French or American lines and a cabinet system of the German or Austrian type. There was also constant argument over the voting system. Some wanted proportional representation, others majority voting. So for six years the political system remained a mixture, neither one nor the other. Meanwhile there was a blurred, conflict-ridden distribution of powers between legislature on the one hand, and the government and presidency on the other. The lower house, the Sejm, was elected by a proportional system and the upper house, the Senate, by simple majority. These dilemmas were largely, if not entirely resolved by the new constitution adopted on 2 April 1997, which won a small majority in a referendum on 25 May. Victory went to cabinet government. The powers of the presidency were reduced and the position of the government strengthened, especially that of the prime minister, who was vested with powers similar to those of a German federal chancellor. The separation of powers is precise. Civil rights are defined and guaranteed in a modern way.

Local government

There has been a democratic system of local government in Poland for six years. Urban and rural authorities are elected by popular ballot and have wide powers and a relatively strong financial base. They collect local taxes and can also raise revenue by letting council-owned premises for commercial and industrial use and by selling land for development. However, the revenues of some authorities fall short of what they need to perform the functions transferred to them from central government. Their responsibilities now extend over primary and secondary education, public health, local utilities and transport, and most highways. Councils that cannot cope financially receive grants from central government.

However, the central authorities have shown signs of reverting to a centralist model of regional policy, favouring direct local-government financing (amounting at present to 82 per cent of their total budget) rather than effective financial autonomy at lower levels. That being so, the current revitalization of government regional policy could lead, paradoxically, not to decentralization but to the reverse. This applies even though implementation of a principle of central government assistance, not domination, with optimization of the scope of local government powers, is an absolute requirement of the democratization process.

Unfortunately, the popularity of the idea of self-government does not match the institutional framework provided for it. Local elections attract scanty interest, and there is little real civil control over local-authority activities. There is fairly frequent alienation of local government, extravagance and waste in management of their finances, and approval of blatantly large salaries and emoluments for mayors and councillors. Corruption scandals occur. In such cases local communities tend to expect central government to intervene rather than take action themselves.

The subject of interregional policy is becoming a key problem of territorial organization of the state. One issue still unresolved is restoration of the district as a key intermediate unit of local government between the commune and the province. Restoration of districts, which existed until the mid-1970s, has many advocates. They argue on practical as well as traditional grounds, saying that most communes are too weak financially and organizationally to discharge important tasks like education and health. However, the move is strongly opposed by the Polish Peasant Party and some of the political right, which want the commune to stay as the main unit of administration. The new constitution left the question open. Introducing greater local autonomy will mean reconsidering the powers of the legislature and executive, and augmenting those of local government, to create rules and regulations that take account of the features, conditions, and size of specific regions.

Social consciousness and the model of political culture

Relics of the warfare concept of politics, a legacy of the mentality fashioned by dictatorial government and the code associated with struggle against such regimes, appear in the tendency to overemphasize ideology in political life. This is manifest primarily in a desire to continue and even intensify the battle against communism. The result is a cleft between the parties descended from those that existed under the socialist system and the "post-communist" parties, with their roots in opposition to "real socialism" ("post-Solidarity"). Both sides have evolved considerably since then, so that the cleft is reflected less in policies than in "genealogy" and axiology, the underlying values professed, notably in attitudes to religion and the Catholic church.

The transfer of competitive politics to an axiological plane is a distinctive feature of political life in Poland. The dichotomy gained significance after 1993, when the Democratic Left Alliance and the Polish Peasant Party, both "post-communist," won the parliamentary elections, and 1995 when Lech Walesa lost the presidential election to Aleksander Kwasniewski. So the political arena and the process of forming a modern democratic political culture are impeded by throwbacks to the period of confrontation between the democratic opposition and the authoritarian communist regime, when political justice and moral rectitude were combined on one side of the divide. Such identification of political with moral justifications today lends the conflicts that would be normal in any democracy a new and essentially undemocratic stamp. They are approached in a spirit of "war." Opponents are held not only to be wrong, but to be wicked and infamous, and one side considers that it possesses a monopoly of good and the other personifies absolute evil. This mentality is at odds with democracy, which is irreconcilable with political or moral monopolies. If axiological claims are allowed to dominate, they prove dysfunctional to the state and society, because they nullify, at least in part, the mechanisms and procedures for orderly contention between policies and options, and the presentation, negotiation, and resolution of these.

Two salient contradictions

The process of transition brought to the surface two salient contradictions. The first was between the nascent new economic system and the social interests deriving from the traditions of "real socialism."

173

As Poland stood on the threshold of transition, almost everybody rejected the old system, symbolically and politically. Later it was also rejected as an ineffective and inefficient system of production. But as a system of welfare provision, social security, and government responsibility for looking after the basic needs of the individual, it continued to be accepted to the end by broad sections of society. Indeed many people expected the transition to bolster these functions of the state, not eliminate them. However, the transition process brought to power political forces that embarked on and continue with a programme of reform that runs counter to these expectations. The reasons for this are understandable and rational, since market economics and abandonment of bureaucratically regulated redistribution offered the only hope of restoring the economy to health and setting it on the path to efficiency. Nevertheless, the contradiction crystallized, and for some time exerted a strong influence on the social and political situation. Although this has not ceased altogether, its impact seems to have lessened in the last two or three years. This is apparent, for instance, in the falling number of social conflicts, strikes, and industrial disputes, which even radical unions appear reluctant to engage in, for fear of not gaining the support of workers.

The second contradiction lies in the political system, for the time being mainly in the spheres of consciousness, culture, and propaganda, but with a tendency to influence the shape and activities of institutions as well. This is the contradiction described earlier, between the logic of democracy and the transfer of political contention and conflicts to the axiological plane. It is a contradiction that seems to be gaining in significance at present.

The political scene

The phenomena just described have crucially affected Poland's political stage, particularly the re-emerging multi-party system. Interestingly, with the one exception of the agrarian movement, it has proved impossible to revive Poland's traditional, historic parties, however distinguished their record of service to the country and the cause of freedom. There has been no renascence of the National Democrats on the right or the Polish Socialist Party on the left, except in a skeletal form, leading a fragile existence with little or no support. The political choices and spectrum are now determined by factors grounded in the experience of more recent decades. The failure of the revived parties to gain popularity is a phenomenon that awaits deeper analysis. The probable explanation is that today's Polish society differs greatly in social structure and political experience from those societies of the first half of the century, so that even the earlier political symbols fail to strike a chord in the popular imagination. Personal symbols may do so, but although Marshal Pilsudski still has a lasting place in most people's national pantheon, no one has succeeded in resuscitating his party.

Nor is there a direct interdependence between social structure and political structure. The party system that has re-emerged since the change of political system exhibits only loose ties with major social groups. In Poland, as in Western Europe, there no longer seems to be a tendency for parties to organize along class lines, with a base in large social groups whose interests they represent. Only among the rural community is there still an attachment to a traditional party, the Polish Peasant Party – probably the only authentic "class" party in contemporary Poland. The constituencies of the other parties are socially differentiated in character. They run on a "catch-all" basis, rather than trying to appeal to specific, distinct social groups. There is some influence, of course, exerted by the degree of contentment or dissatisfaction with transition, but it is not a decisive factor, or at least not the only or principal one.

Most analysts of Polish politics find it difficult to classify parties in the traditional way, into left, right, conservative, or radical. Many parties claiming to be on the left, even the Social Democrats, are influenced predominantly by advocates of economic liberalism. By contrast, parties that describe themselves as right wing show leanings towards etatist socialism. They favour protection of government-subsidized, state-owned industry, and show hostility to privatization, corporatism in economic governance, and so on. Roughly speaking, liberals, conservatives, proponents of a redistributive state, albeit non-communist, quasi-socialist ones, can be found in all parties in varying proportions. Even attitudes to the church, a preference for secularism, or for some form of denominational state, are not clear distinguishing features. Supporters of both coexist in all parties except the secularist Social Democrats and the clericalist Movement for Poland's Reconstruction.

So what defines Poland's political structure today? What makes the political situation so polarized, so that the parties or camps fight each other with a fierceness bordering on what Adam Michnik has called a "cold civil war?" The battle lines are drawn by at least three structures patterned by history.

The first, still discernible though now fading and the weakest, derives from the more distant past of the early post-war years. It echoes the divisions between those who in one way or another accepted the new system of socialism and those who continued to resist it, even fruitlessly taking up arms. These divisions have survived most obviously in bitter contention between several rival organizations of veterans, but they also seem to be responsible for a geographical differentiation of political opinion that otherwise looks hard to explain. In all the elections the south-east and east of the country have voted for decidedly anti-communist, nationalist-Catholic options, while central and western Poland has favoured so-called post-communist or moderate post-Solidarity parties. The point here is that the south-east and east of Poland saw the fiercest struggle in 1944–1947, bordering on civil war, over the shape of the system to come.

The second political structure, deeper and more clear-cut, derives from the historic division into what are conventionally called the post-Solidarity and post-People's Poland camps, as represented in the June 1989 election. Their relative strengths have changed and become more evenly balanced, the post-Solidarity camp having lost ground, but the cleft remains. On the post-Solidarity side, Inka Slodkowska, a sociologist (writing in *Rzeczpospolita*, 30 May 1997), placed the Movement for Poland's Reconstruction (ROP) on the extreme wing and Solidarity Electoral Action (AWS) on the more moderate wing, while on the other side stand the Democratic Left Alliance (SLD – the coalition over which the Social Democrats preside) and the Polish Peasants Party (PSL). The Freedom Union (UW) leans towards the post-Solidarity camp, while the Union of Labour (UP) stands between the two. There are considerable differences within these camps, which are distinguished by several clear-cut, emotionally charged options: attitudes to People's Poland and its legacy, to privatization and denationalization, to screening politicians for connections with the old secret police, and to the Catholic church. The argument is also about specific issues. These include acknowledgement of post-war continuity or rejection of the People's Republic as a foreign regime, restitution of the pre-communist pattern of property ownership or construction of private ownership from the basics, recognition of full legal equality or curtailment of the rights, including some property rights, of a smaller or larger group identified with People's Poland, and finally, submission primarily to the tenets of religion, "natural law," before the law of the state.

It is worth quoting Inka Slodkowska again:

The above factors divide the actors in Polish politics as deeply, for example, as the American political stage was divided by the slavery issue a hundred years ago, or is split in half by an abortion-related conflict today. In other words, a very important part in the Polish transformation process is played by symbolic premises of political action and value systems.

On these historically and axiologically conditioned structures are superimposed divisions derived from attitudes to economic and political transition, modernization, and specific policies. As a rule, all parties appear to embrace a common "core": acceptance of market-oriented reforms, accession to European structures, and respect for human rights and democracy. Such declarations are standard features of all their official programmes, although the picture looks a little different in political journalism, and even more during election campaigns. The ostensible consensus and unanimity of the programme statements prove more apparent than real when set against political practice. Considerable light on the actual pattern of preferences over reform and modernization was shed by the constitutional referendum of 25 May 1997.

Thanks to the referendum, Poland has at last a new and democratic constitution. It is worth noting that this is only the second Polish constitution ever to be adopted by unquestionably democratic procedures. (The first was in March 1921. The same cannot be said of the constitutions of May 1791 or April 1935, and still less of those of the Duchy of Warsaw (1807) or the Polish Kingdom (1816), which were imposed by foreign monarchs.) About 43 per cent of the electorate voted in the referendum. Supporters of the new constitution outnumbered opponents by less than 7 percentage points.

The results of the referendum suggest a number of conclusions. Political Poland continues to be split almost in half, as it was in the 1993 parliamentary elections (although this was not reflected in the distribution of seats) and the 1995 presidential election. This has less to do with attitudes to specific issues than with historical symbols. However, confirmation that the "genealogical" cleft remained was not the only message of the referendum. Far more important were the new signals it sent. There were two parties that decried the constitution and campaigned for its rejection: the Movement for Poland's Reconstruction and Solidarity Electoral Action. If the more substantial arguments of the constitution's opponents are separated from the vote-catching chaff, it becomes easier to grasp the position of the groupings that lost the referendum, in spite of the blessing and active support of the church hierarchy. The fiercest attacks were directed at the provisions that prepared the way for real, as opposed to apparent integration with European structures. These even prompted cries of treason. There was an equally vehement assault on a clause that avoids making a specific pronouncement about the legality of abortion and leaves the decision to parliament. There were loud calls for a declaration that "natural law" (the tenets of religion) should take precedence over law promulgated by the state. Other demands included replacement of effective privatization with a semblance of it, labelled "property ownership for all," and introduction of some corporatist elements into the system, by transferring some parliamentary powers to government-union negotiating bodies. So the referendum campaign revealed that most post-Solidarity groupings, now associated either with the Movement for Poland's Reconstruction or Solidarity Electoral Action, challenged vital parts of the democratic changes since 1989, including market-based economic structures and integration with European institutions. It is hard to say how much of this opposition sprang from parochial fundamentalism and how much from hopes of wooing voters disenchanted by the transition and fearful of modernization.

However, the "genealogical" cleft was not total this time. Among the architects of the constitution and its champions in the referendum were two important post-Solidarity parties, the Freedom Union and the Union of Labour, whose leaders had been the intellectual spearhead of the camp in the 1981–1990 period. This may presage the end of the political dichotomy that has troubled Poland for the past seven years. That would raise hopes of a normality and modernity in politics and behaviour, which would be welcome because the public seems profoundly weary of the "cold civil war" that some of the post-Solidarity side have been intent on waging. Most observers agree in attributing the low election polls to this weariness and distaste.

Feeling that the church hierarchy was on their side, the opponents of the constitution also expected a declaration of support from Pope John Paul II when he made his June pilgrimage to Poland. They were disappointed in this, which must have been distressing for the politically more vocal bishops. What the Pope told the huge crowds that flocked to hear him was mainly of a religious and moral nature. The Pope's position on matters of doctrine was precise and traditional, but there was no hint of a crusade. The keynote was kindly persuasion. Addressing himself to the bishops, he warned against church involvement in politics and urged *"discernimento"* and acceptance of "what may be valid in any piece of criticism." In Cracow he appealed to his audience to ensure that the "Polish deed" did not strike anyone "with hatred and contempt" and united rather than divided people.

Changes after the 1997 parliamentary elections

The parliamentary elections on 21 September 1997 aroused a relatively moderate level of interest among voters. Only 48 per cent of the electorate went to the polls. This compares with turn-outs of 52 per cent in 1993, and 68 per cent in the second round of the 1995 presidential election. The swings were small. The right-wing parties, now united into the Solidarity Electoral Action (AWS) bloc, polled 4.5 million votes in 1991, 4 million in 1993, and 4.4 million in 1997. The Freedom Union (UW, resulting from a merger of the Democratic Union and the Liberal Democratic Congress) gained 2.2 million votes in 1991, 2 million in 1993, and 1.75 million in 1997. The Democratic Left Alliance (SLD) received 1.35 million votes in 1991, 2.8 million in 1993, and 3.55 million in 1997; the Polish Peasants Party (PSL) 1 million in 1991, 2.15 million in 1993, and 0.95 million in 1997; and the Union of Labour (UP), which now has no representatives in parliament, 0.3 million in 1991, 1 million in 1993, and 0.6 million in 1997.

These figures show that support for the right has remained more or less unchanged. The SLD has been collecting a steadily rising number of votes. The position of the PSL, Poland's only class-based party, is shaky, and the same applies to the UP, which represents the post-Solidarity left. All in all, the electoral popularity of the right, the centre, and the left (totalling the votes of the SLD and UP) has remained at roughly the same as in 1993. There was a slight swing of 3–4 per cent to the right, mainly at the expense of the centre (the UW and PSL).

Despite the stability of the voting patterns, the political stage has been transformed quite radically. The SLD/PSL coalition lost power to an alliance of post-Solidarity parties, mainly because of the damage sustained by the PSL in the polls. The AWS owed its success primarily to the fact that there was just a single list of right-wing candidates. If the groups of which it is composed had also contested the 1993 election as a bloc, they would have beaten the winner, the SLD, by a substantial majority (probably by 30–40 seats), and been able to form a centre-right coalition with the UW or the PSL.

The causes of the PSL setback are unclear. Some observers attribute the disaster to the party leadership's policy for two years of playing a dual role, as co-ruler and as opposition. Other analysts look deeper, and see it as a reflection of the waning appeal of an agrarian, class-based party. Economic and cultural changes in rural society have left the peasantry clearly differentiated into a middle class of farmers and a stratum of agricultural labourers. Rural votes in the last elections were divided almost equally between the AWS, the SLD, and the PSL.

The marked decline in support for the Union of Labour may show that voters on the left are no longer put off by the SLD's postcommunist label, so that the demand for a left-wing party without such a stigma is dwindling.

The outcome of the elections has left a tripartite political structure. The right has a decidedly Catholic, largely populist complexion. There is a social-democratic left of ex-communist ancestry, and a liberal democratic centre, the UW – the weakest of the three, but still capable of holding the balance. Despite losing votes and seats, the UW strengthened its position. Without it, the AWS would have been unable to form a stable government, which would soon have meant new elections.

Another important conclusion from the post-election analyses is that class and related alignments are tending to decrease among voters. The constituencies of the two biggest groupings, the AWS and the SLD, have social structures. The AWS commands slightly more support in big cities and among workers in state-owned industry, while the SLD is a little stronger among educated voters and in small towns. The UW recruits mainly from the professional sector. The middle class is politically divided among all three parties. A differentiation among voters stronger than social background, age, or education is ideology, attitudes to the past (the period of communist rule), and susceptibility to the influence of the church. One consequence is a marked territorial distribution of electoral strengths. Eastern and southern Poland, where the traditional, rural model of religious belief survives, voted overwhelmingly for the AWS. Regions that are more secularized as a result of migration processes (western Poland) or advancement of civilization (Poznania, Pomerania) were SLD strongholds. The UW proved to be a primarily metropolitan party. Young voters showed no distinct preferences.

One intriguing feature was the low turn-out, of which the SLD seems to have been the main casualty. At any rate that is the message of surveys conducted among people who failed to vote. Contributing factors were complacency and a feeble campaign. There was a prevailing belief in the SLD that the booming economy ruled out the possibility of defeat for a party in power. Insufficient account was taken of imponderable factors, and of the considerable influence over many decades of the right and the Catholic church among the sections of society interested in politics. There was a pre-war saying: *Polonus homo naturaliter endecianus est* – the Pole is by nature a national (Christian) democrat. Analysis of the non-voters in elections seems to indicate that apart from the educated and professional sector, which voted in greater numbers than other groups, the country at large – the working class and peasantry – showed a fairly even distribution of abstentions. The turn-out among young voters was lower than average.

The left could not count in this election campaign on any major support from the media, except for the weekly *Nie* (circulation 500,000) and the daily *Trybuna* (100,000). The strongest media backing went to the UW (public television, the biggest private station Polsat, and the best-selling newspaper, Gazeta Wyborcza), but this did not prove to be a great advantage. It must therefore be assumed that the assets which brought the AWS victory were the efficient organization provided by its trade-union core and the support of the Catholic church, notably the militantly clerical Radio Maria. Potent opinion-making centres capable of exerting a tangible, lasting influence on the public have yet to emerge in Poland. The decisive factors continue to be forces and traditions that go back many years or decades: the church, the legacy of the communist period, and the Solidarity tradition. Now that the heirs of the communist period have had four years in government and to some extent spent themselves, and the day has dawned for the Solidarity myth, there may be a turning-point approaching, and beyond it, the appearance of significant centres that aim to climb out of the ideological trenches and develop social and political thinking grounded in the realities of the present. However, this prospect is at least two or three years ahead.

For the time being, politics will hinge on the relationship between the AWS and the UW. The AWS is a mixed bag, representing a wide array of interests, from liberal free-marketers to people with narrower, more nationalist horizons. The alliance includes many members of the groups that have suffered most under the new regime – miners, farmers, factory workers. They played a strong part in the overthrow of communism, and then found their standard of living falling. The only common denominator in the AWS continues to be powerful anti-communist sentiments, which find expression in ill-defined plans for "decommunization" and burying the legacy of the post-war period. On all other issues the AWS is racked by conflicting tendencies. One powerful influence is the trade-union wing, which has a distinctly populist hue. At the opposite extreme is a far weaker wing of economic liberals, represented by the 100 Movement and the Conservative People's Party. A strong and active force is the nationalist-Catholic current, with unmistakable leanings towards religious fundamentalism, represented by the Christian National Union and a large group of legislators associated with Radio Maria. A separate group consists of supporters of ex-president Lech Walesa and the former Centre Alliance. There are Euro-enthusiasts, and a sizeable batch of Eurosceptics. The leader, Marian Krzaklewski, well aware of the latent centrifugal tendencies, wanted to transform the AWS into a political party with a clear-cut hierarchical structure. He was unable to do this before the elections, and many observers doubt that he ever will.

Unlike the AWS, the UW has a well-defined identity. It is committed to parliamentary democracy and economic liberalism, and unqualified in its support for Europe. Objectively its liberal politics mean it represents the interests of entrepreneurs, professionals, and other sectors of the broadly defined middle class.

The coalition with the UW was forced on the AWS (for want of any other way of forming a government) and concluded with difficulty, in the teeth of a large section of the AWS. This coalition has brought to the fore the "better," more democratic and modern part of the AWS, but it has intensified its internal strains. The positions of the AWS and UW differ profoundly on almost every issue: vision of the state, macroeconomic policy, attitudes to privatization and foreign investment, policy towards agriculture, trade policy, European integration, clauses in the constitution relating to values, and many other points.

Of course, there are a number of shared objectives, such as membership of NATO, decentralization of the state and reform of local-government jurisdiction (although here too, the policies are still only declamatory). However, there is no indication of sufficiently strong foundations for efficient, conflict-free government in the longer run. In many crucial areas – taxation, education, welfare provisions, or the extent of intervention – the basic interests of the two coalition partners, at any rate in the short and mid-term, are self-evidently at variance. It will be an awkward, conflict-ridden coalition, forever on the brink of crisis. Withdrawals from the AWS are possible, which would strengthen the UW's position in the coalition, but enhance the voice of the parliamentary opposition, the SLD. Also possible are attempts instigated by the fundamentalists and their church patrons to turn the UW into a vassal. That would augur badly for the democratic system in Poland, by initiating an authoritarian, fundamentalist drift in public policy that would threaten human rights, and more generally, the rule of law. For the moment there is no way of estimating how real or how strong such dangers are.

The area in which the firmest predictions can be made is the economic outlook, for two reasons: (i) the UW is unlikely to make concessions on economic policy. Its leader, Leszek Balcerowicz, is a man with a strong personality and a high international reputation in the field. (ii) The economy has achieved a marked degree of autonomy from politics. It would not be easy to 'spoil' this by political interference. There will be a favourable climate in the new parliament for decentralizing the state, by creating a new, intermediate tier of local government, and larger regional jurisdictions than the present provinces. Such reforms are favoured not only by the UW, but by much of the AWS and the opposition SLD. Implementation of these plans – lent urgency because local-government elections are due in June 1998 – would greatly bolster the economy and the regions, and create barriers to warping the democratic system.

Conclusion

The transition process in Poland has reached the stage where the economic and political spheres have to a large extent become autonomous. Political tremors and battles have only a slight impact on the economy, whose development is driven by the market. The democratic system has gained solid institutional foundations, but there is weakness in the underlying consciousness and culture of society, where ambivalent attitudes prevail. Freedom is universally cherished as an inherent value, but there remains a strong current of etatist sympathy and expectations of official intervention whenever difficulties are encountered. Majority rule is often seen as majority *Diktat*, and respect for the rights of dissidents, those who think differently (e.g. non-believers), or of various minorities is not firmly entrenched. Many social groups are still easily swayed by demagogy. The level of political cultivation is quite low, even in the political class and the media. This means there are still threats to democracy, especially from populists and their etatist allies, and of sporadic outbreaks of anarchic behaviour and local unrest. If tendencies like these become dominant and assert a strong influence on parliamentary alignments and government policy in the longer run, there will be a danger of economic distortions, a halt to privatization, and a rise in government expenditure, and consequently in the budget deficit and inflation.

A powerful barrier to such eventualities is the influence exerted on the Polish situation by the international environment, especially Western Europe and the United States, and the prospect of integration with NATO and the EU.

References

Wnuk-Lipinski, Edmund, ed. (1995), *After Communism, A Multidisciplinary Approach to Radical Social Change*, Warsaw: Polish Academy of Sciences.

Kuklinski, Antoni, ed. (1997), *European Space, Polish Space*, Vol. II, Warsaw: Rewasz.

Lukovski, Wojciech, and Konstanty Wojtaszczyk, eds. (1996), *Reform and Transformation in Eastern Europe*, Warsaw: Elipsa.

Baczko, Tadeusz, ed. (1996), *The Second Stage of Polish Economic Transformation: Transformation Policy*, Warsaw: Polish Scientific Publishers.

Szklarski, Bogdan (1997), *Semi-public Democracy, Articulation of Interests and Systemic Transformation*, Warsaw: Polish Scientific Publishers.

Jablonski, Andrzej, and Gerd Meyer, eds. (1996), *The Political Culture of Poland in Transition*, Wroclaw: Wroclaw University.

Golebiowski, Janusz, ed. (1994), *Transforming the Polish Economy*, Vols. I and II, Warsaw: World Economy Research Institute.

10

Issues and experiences in the practice of democratization: Models and paradigms

Iván Vitányi

I fully agree with those who say that the notion of "democracy" is not homogeneous or unambiguous. There is no single connection between the process of democratization and of the spread of the markets or economic performances. There are various kinds of democracies, in space and in time. The traditional French version of democracy differs from the English one, and both differ from the American tradition, analysed initially by de Tocqueville. The democracy of the last century differs strongly from democracy in the first half of this century, which in turn differs from the democracy of the decades since the Second World War. The Eastern-Central European changes produce not one but many configurations and patterns of democracy. The differences in institutions and in social structures also play a role in the patterns of transition to the market economy.

I think Robert Dahl aptly described the present phase as polyarchy. It is the highest stage so far in the development of the political system of human society, but it is not the final stage of democracy as such. It is a well-organized type of representative democracy, marked by a multi-party political system, in which parliamentary and municipal elections take place every four or five years.

Who are the main actors in this polyarchic system?

185

Political practice and political science traditionally distinguish three plus two major political trends, movements, and directions. These are conservatism (including various national, Christian, and other variants of it), liberalism, and social democracy, with the addition of the extreme right and left. The first three are central to politics in all the Euro-Atlantic countries, a kind of "political trinity" embracing the establishment, whose constituents normally succeed each other in office. The extremes set up camp and attack from outside the bulwarks of the establishment, aiming to force a radical transformation of the whole political structure.

It has been said that the political system is in a frozen state, that for several decades, the protagonists themselves have not changed, they have simply changed their positions.

East-Central Europe and the democratic perspective

The long-term future of the East-Central European region will be decided in the next 10–15 years. The ultimate direction will result not from a single decision, but from a series of decisions, in the context of a variety of processes.

These processes have been going on for decades, or even a millennium. They have hitherto represented a set of unresolved questions lying at the heart of Europe, in its geographical centre. Present-day Europe is customarily seen to consist of a centre and a periphery and semi-periphery, distinguished by indices of economic and social development. It should be remembered that the borderline between the two territories had evolved by the end of the eighth century – it coincides with the border of Western Christianity, of Charlemagne's empire. Furthermore, it was a thousand years ago, at the end of the tenth century, that the rulers of the Central European countries – Poland, Bohemia, and Hungary – adhered to Western Christianity and received royal crowns from the Pope in Rome. The emerging countries of the region in turmoil, such as Croatia, Slovenia, Lithuania, had the same intention.

The situation has remained equivocal ever since. In more propitious periods of history, the manifest historical intention seemed to have been realized – these countries became increasingly integrated into European life. Then came other periods when this prospect receded into the distance. After the discovery of America, the region found itself outside the main thrust of development. At the same time, conquests by empires that represented an earlier phase of development – Mongols, Tatars, and Ottomans – set the region back from what it had already achieved.

The twentieth century repeated the historical pattern of several previous centuries, in a magnified form, dividing the two areas of Europe from each other by the Iron Curtain. The Western European, or rather Euro-Atlantic region has undergone, during the last half-century, one of the biggest spurts of development in its history. This has created a modern economy with a welfare state and imbedded pluralist democracy and a constitutional system. Meanwhile Eastern and Central Europe, under Soviet domination, experienced a command economy and dictatorial rule that consolidated its peripheral backwardness.

The historic turning-point of 1989–1990 has offered the countries of the former Soviet bloc another chance to try to integrate into European democracy. It is not yet clear whether the effort will succeed, and if so to what extent it will be fruitful.

The transition, which embraces political, economic, social, psychological, institutional, national, and international changes, is not a unidirectional or homogeneous process. The different chapters of this volume underline the three main distinct processes within the whole. First, there is the *political transition*, the change of the regime. This takes a relatively short time. Establishing the institutional framework for a democratic system – free elections, multi-party pluralism, a parliamentary system, elected municipalities, legitimate government, a president, a constitutional court, and so on – has proved to be a rapid process in most transition countries, especially those with some previous democratic traditions. However, it may be several years before this framework operates smoothly and appropriately, according to the norms and values of Western-type democratic states. The second process is the *economic transition*, the change from a command economy, controlled by the single ruling party, to a market economy operating with a money mechanism, with the absolute majority of private ownership. This is more difficult and complicated. It likewise includes establishing institutions, but it requires major changes in redistributive systems, in management, in domestic and international competitiveness, and in the role of the state as a source of income and services, and as a direct participant in the economy. Finally, the third process is the *cultural change* and the *development of a civil society*, which takes an even longer time, although the duration should not be overestimated. The special role and relatively high level of cultivation in most East-Central European countries together form one of their main characteristics. The cultures of these societies are in a better position and at a higher level of development than their economies. These countries have failed to catch up with the countries at the centre in economic development, but have managed to approach more closely to them in culture. To give a single example, the region was the birthplace of the European avant-garde revival of the arts and culture that took place at the beginning of the century.

One question remains, however. Is political, economic, and cultural transition as a whole possible for the Central and Eastern European countries? Can there be a transition to a truly European economy of a Western European standard, to what can be called a welfare or post-welfare, modern or post-modern, post-industrial, or neo-capitalist society and economy? Or will it only be a transition from one form of everlasting underdevelopment, to another form of underdevelopment (to borrow the phrase of André Gunder Frank). This question affects Europe as a whole, not just the countries concerned.

The *political* process, on which this paper focuses, will be crucial to determining the path of the changes. So what are the alternatives? In fact there are two strategies, two possible paths.

The first is systematic adaptation to the Euro-Atlantic system, while only on the margin of it so far, but already within it, so that the same conflicts and problems will emerge as the central countries have experienced during the crisis of the welfare state.

The second way is an alternative raised repeatedly from either the left or the right. This means finding a different royal road that evades the problems of world capitalism, but would also leave the region to wallow in the misery of its small-scale capitalism. (Historically, this second way is referred to as the "third road.")

The choice is not a symmetrical one. The first alternative is a genuine possibility, although scarcely achievable in reality. The second, of evading world capitalism, is just a pipe-dream, although the misery of dependent small-scale capitalism will be real indeed.

The governments and political parties of what was the Soviet bloc function within the field of these possibilities. Due to their specific situation, they do not choose between the alternatives according to the traditional European divisions of political thinking. The first way – joining the system – may be accomplished by liberals, social democrats, or conservatives. Advocates of the second way can be found among conservatives and socialists of the right or the left. (Liberals are least numerous among them, or wrongly style themselves liberals, such as Zhirinovsky in Russia.)

One of the most interesting (and for many people unexpected) phenomena is the strong political presence of successors to the previous state-parties in the region. This is a general characteristic of the transformation whose causes it would take more detailed analysis to reveal.

The development and present role of the successors to the Soviet-type "communist" parties had two courses before them. One was to make the transition to European social democracy, join the Socialist International, and adapt to Western Europe. That was the course chosen by the Hungarian and Polish parties. (The difference is that the Hungarian party has been in cooperation with the liberals, while the Polish social democrats and liberals are opposed to each other.) There the former communist parties were able to fill the place of social democracy, although there had been strong orthodox social democratic parties in those countries before the communist period. So what happened? In each case a strong reform wing emerged within the official ruling party during the late 1980s, and this readopted the social-democratic tradition. By 1990 the reformers had developed integral relations with various strata in society and gained some routine experience of technocratic leadership. On the other hand, the remnants of the old social democratic parties, who had survived Stalinism, were unable to develop a concept and strategy adequate for present-day social democracy.

The second way was followed by the Serbian, Romanian, and Slovak ruling parties (under Milosević, Iliescu, and Meciar) and by some others. They represent the second strategy with a more or less national character. They rely on the power structure of previous decades, and their covert single-party system departs from the main line of development.

How does this fit in with the European political structure, the trinity of main political forces? Will this trinity of liberalism, social democracy, and conservatism last forever? Will our grandchildren still be facing the same choice? This is the great question-mark over our age. For the time being there is no answer, or at least, nothing can be proved or falsified, but certain tendencies are becoming apparent.

To answer the question entails analysing the development and decline of the *welfare state*, the most comprehensive paradigm of the Euro-Atlantic political and economic system in the last 50 years, which was not just liberal, social democratic, or conservative, but a combination of all three.

The history of the welfare state had three phases.

The first phase was the classical pattern, after the Second World War, whose founding fathers included the liberal Keynes, the social democrat Erlander and the conservative Erhardt. The welfare state was a compromise and an alliance, or as Oskar Lafontaine has put it, a contradictory cooperation between capitalism and social democracy. To borrow the formula of Immanuel Wallerstein and Adam Przeworski, the workers reconciled themselves to capitalism, and the capitalists to democracy.

The same can be said of the second phase, when a new paradigm was created in response to an impending crisis of the welfare state. This Hayek-Friedman concept was usually called neo-liberalism, but a conservative version of it. Who put it into practice? It was not only liberals, but conservatives (Thatcher and Reagan), social democrats (Gonzales), and even the extreme right (Pinochet). This paradigm has since lost the magic attached to it (mainly by the liberals). So there either has to be found a plank between the two models, or there has to be a new model.

I see two main alternatives developing. These do not entirely coincide with the political trinity, but intersect its borders, as Seymour Martin Lipset notes in the final study of a selection published in memory of Schumpeter, under the title *Capitalism, Socialism and Democracy Revisited*. There are two opposing poles. For one, the most important thing is freedom, democracy, and equality, and for the other, preserving the status quo, for fear of imbalance caused by progress.

The Euro-Atlantic world has recently entered a third phase: the crisis of the welfare state. The cooperation of corporative capitalism with corporative social democracy has been ended, or rather cancelled by the growing power of the new corporative economy.

The key question is the *relation between corporatism and democracy*, where there are again two possible alternatives: (i) the wider, well-organized, growing technocratic power of the transnational corporations brings less democracy, merely a formal democracy; (ii) more autonomy and flexibility are gained in an open, civil society, with strong democracy and containment and control of corporatism.

The level and form of democracy developed after the Second World War, within the welfare states of the Euro-Atlantic countries, form the pinnacle of the world's political development so far, but why should it be the end? Why would we consider it a perfection and fulfilment of development, an end of history? For there are ways forward or backward from here.

What can be said about the first paradigm: more corporatism, less democracy? The world economy is kept under such tight control by the transnational corporations that it allows more organized and active, and at the same time more centralized, power systems to emerge than ever before. *When Corporations Rule the World* is the title of a book by David L. Korten, in which he argues and proves that they really do that. The new technical revolutions diminish the role of work. (Will society run out of work, asks Hannah Arendt?) So the threat of work is not so strong. On the other hand, the traditional means of suppression are not needed, for new mechanisms for imposing uniformity and domesticating thinking and behaviour have been developed. Benjamin Barber called this new mechanism the McWorld (generalizing the idea of McDonalds). Its main techniques are "infotainments," a new mixture of information and entertainment that the new technical opportunities help with penetrating society and superseding the values of true culture. (The McWorld has counterparts in Saint Jihad, various kinds of fundamentalism, in which a new type of one-dimensional, authoritarian thinking emerges and rules.)

The McWorld does not mean the repeal of democracy, simply its degradation into a façade. Behind the façade of polyarchy's spectacular choices, there are well-organized, corporative centres working in the real spaces of decisions, and they have the final word. That is how democracy can often descend into what Philipp Schmitter so aptly describes as "democrature."

Can people live under such a system? They can, because for most of them it offers a fairly appropriate standard of living, and it not only dictates the necessary quality of life, but provides it. This kind of system does not need coercion. The McWorld of culture and behaviour is a better and less expensive means of imposing authority than weapons or prisons.

Here we have to return to East-Central Europe, to pose the following question. How has it been possible for the social democratic successors of the old Stalinist ("communist") state-parties to use their previous experience so well under the present conditions of transition to democracy?

An answer to this can now be given, because certain late communist states (especially Poland and Hungary) had already become half-corporative systems, usually known as "soft" dictatorships. When countries undergoing democratic transformation want to join the Euro-Atlantic system, if possible as equal members, they have to integrate themselves into the Western corporative system. Letting in multinationals (which then play the most important role in economic advancement) is not the only requirement. The countries must also imbibe the forms of management and social behaviour that organically belong to them, and these are best comprehended by those who already have experience of corporatism, if of a different kind.

This contains the intrinsic paradox in the countries of East-Central Europe. If they want to leave the zone of dependent capitalism and join the Euro-Atlantic system, they will need some corporatism, in about the quantity they already have. However, if they acquire more than the optimum measure, they will become dependent, and even as NATO members, consigned to the zone of semi-periphery.

Is there a way out of this difficulty? Hardly, for just one country or one region alone. The only way out is to fall in with general Western European and North American development lines that seek to gain the same objectives. So is the second paradigm – more democracy, less corporatism – a realistic alternative?

There is a wide choice of terms to denominate the second paradigm. It has been called an *open society* (Karl Popper), *participatory democracy, strong democracy* (Benjamin Barber), *civil democracy* (André Gunder Frank), *societal democracy* (Norberto Bobbio), *good society* (John Kenneth Galbraith), *flexible society* (Stuart Holland), and *transparent society* (Giuseppe Vattimo). These various expressions describe a society in which increasing numbers of the population take part in decision-making, not just in elections every four or five years, but constantly. This is a society in which democracy has control over corporations and can even limit their power. Furthermore, people can fulfil themselves culturally, not succumb to a torrent of "infotainment," and the crisis of the welfare state is resolved by developing a *welfare society*.

This situation is getting closer and closer to the critical point. Adepts of democracy hope that both solutions are possible by equal forces and that chances are also equal. Real analyses of the situation do not produce so optimistic a picture. Not only democracy (opposed to dictatorship) but corporatism strengthened in the general euphoria that followed the collapse of the Soviet Union. The last decade of the century is theirs – it belongs to the corporations. This means we are at the crossroads, and an answer has to be given by the next century.

Every political movement faces alternatives on this question, not just as a chance, but as a necessity. Every country and political trend must respond. Adherents of both paradigms are found in every political trend – liberalism, social democracy, Christian democracy, conservatism. Can a global consciousness develop, as Yehudi Menuhin, Erwin Laszlo, the Dalai Lama, and others declared in the Manifesto of the Budapest Club in 1997?

The situation offers the East-Central European countries a special, historic opportunity. There have often been occasions in history, at the beginning of a new epoch and a new, developing system of relations, when countries neither in the first line nor very much behind it, neither part of the centre nor on the periphery, played a decisive role in forming the future. (That happened, for instance, to the United States of America during the nineteenth century.)

The reason is clear. Catching up can offer the chance to create something new, and if the circumstances are right, this may be less difficult than transforming structures deeply rooted in the past. However, the countries of East-Central Europe seem for the time being not to be able to take advantage of this situation, because of the difficulties rooted in the dual tasks of the transition, the consequences of the ethnic divisions of the region, the weakness of the institutional and political capabilities in managing the evolving problems in an ethically and socially acceptable way, and to a certain extent because of the traditional and new sources of nationalism in the region.

References

Arendt, Hannah (1987), *On Revolution*, London: Penguin Books.

Barber, Benjamin (1984), *Strong Democracy*, Los Angeles: California Univerity Press.

Barber, Benjamin (1990), *Jihad vs. McWorld*, New York: Random House.

Dahl, Robert Allan (1990), *After the Revolution*, New Haven, Conn.: Yale University Press.

Dahrendorf, Ralf (1996), *Betrachtungen über die Revolution in Europa*, Stuttgart: Deutsche Verlag Anstalt.

Frank, André Gunder, and Fuentes, Marta (1990), "Civil Democracy: Civil Movements in Recent World History," in *Social Movements and the World-System*, New York: Monthly Revue Press.

Galbraith, John Kenneth (1996), *The Good Society*, Boston-New York, Houghton Mifflin.

Holland, Stuart (1993), *The European Imperative: Economic and Social Cohesion in the 1990s*, New York: Spokesman.

Korten, David C. (1995), *When Corporations Rule the World*, West Hartford, Conn.: Kumarian Press and San Francisco: Berrett-Koehler.

Lafontaine, Oskar (1989), *Der andere Fortschritt*. Hamburg: Hoffmann und Campe.

Lipset, Seymour Martin (1993), "Concluding Reflections," in *Capitalism, Socialism and Democracy Revisited*, Baltimore: The Johns Hopkins University Press.

Popper, Karl R. (1945), *The Open Society and its Enemies*, London: George Rout-
ledge.
Schmitter, Philip C. (1974), "Still the Century of Corporatism?," *Revue of Politics*,
No. 36.
Schmitter, Philip C., and Lynn, Karl Terry (1991), "What Democracy is ... and is
Not," in *Journal of Democracy*, No. 3.
Vattimo, Gianni (1992), *The Transparent Society*, Baltimore: The Johns Hopkins
University Press.

Contributors

Dr. Jacques Baudot, Lawyer, Political Scientist. Currently Senior Adviser to the Government of Denmark for the follow-up to the World Summit for Social Development held in Copenhagen in March 1995. Dr. Baudot served in the United Nations from 1970 to 1996 in various positions including Director of the Budget, Controller, and Coordinator of the preparation of the Social Summit.

Prof. Oleg T. Bogomolov, Economist, Member of the Russian Academy of Sciences. Honorary Director (former Director) of the Institute for International Economic and Political Studies (Russian Academy of Sciences), Adviser to the Russian Academy of Sciences, former Member of the State Duma (Parliament).

Prof. Janus Golebiowski, Economist, University Professor in International Relations and Director of the World Economy Research Institute at the

Warsaw School of Economics. Guest Lecturer at several universities in Europe, Asia, and the United States. From 1981 to 1988 Senior Programme Officer of the United Nations University, Tokyo.

Prof. Ivan Grdešić, Political Scientist, Associate Professor in the Faculty of Political Science at the University of Zagreb. Dr. Grdesic specializes in policy analysis, decision-making, local government, and electoral studies. He is currently President of the Croatian Political Science Association.

Prof. György Jenei, Sociologist, Associate Professor at the Department of Public Policy and Management (Budapest University of Economic Sciences, Hungary). Dr. Jenei teaches Public Policy Process and Comparative Social Policy, and is a member of the Steering Committee at the European Group of Public Administration.

195

Prof. Kálman Kulcsár, Lawyer, Sociologist, Member of the Hungarian Academy of Sciences and Chairman of the Social Sciences Section of the Academy. Former Director of the Institute of Political Sciences and former Minister of Justice in the Hungarian Government.

Prof. Youri M. Matseiko, Political Scientist, Senior Research Fellow, Institute of World Economy and International Relations Professor of the Diplomatic Academy of Ukraine. Doctor of Sciences, Envoy Extraordinary and Plenipotentiary, formerly Deputy Ambassador to the United Nations.

Prof. Ján Morovic, Electronic Engineer, Advisor to Minister for Education of the Slovak Republic, former President and Founder of the City University Bratislava where he is currently responsible for curricula development. He has been working as a Research Fellow in the International Institute for Applied System Analysis, and was a member of Parliament in the Federal Assembly of the Czech and Slovak Federative Republic.

Prof. Mihály Simai, Economist, Member of the Hungarian Academy of Sciences, Research Professor in the Institute for World Economics of the Hungarian Academy of Sciences, Professor of Budapest University. Former Member and Chairman of the Council of the United Nations University and former Director of the World Institute for Development Economics of the United Nations University.

Prof. Iván Vitányi, Sociologist, writer, University Professor in the Institute of Sociology of the Budapest University, former Director of the Institute of Culture of the Hungarian Academy of Sciences, currently a member of the Hungarian Parliament and Chairman of its Committee of Culture.

196

Index

life expectancy, Russia 81
Lipset, Seymour Martin 190
Lipsky, M. 71
Lithuania 186
living standards *see* standards of living
local government
  Hungary 149–51
  Poland 171–2
  Slovakia 130
  Ukraine 100
Lowi, Theodore 124n.2
Lukoil 84
Lutheranism 61

Maastricht Treaty 33
Madison, James 43
mafia
  Poland 168
  Russia 51, 90
majority voting 58n.12
  Poland 171, 183
  see also first-past-the-post system
manager buy-outs (MBO), Croatia 118
managerialism
  civil servants 61, 72
  and legalism, dichotomy between 60
  markets, role of 42
  Poland 167
Marković, Ante 113
Marx, Karl 38
Matsukata, Masayoshi 64
Mazowiecki, Tadeusz 170
McWorld 191
Meciar, Vladimir 189
Meciars' Party 134
media
  Commonwealth of Independent States 86
  Croatia 115, 123
  Poland 169, 181, 184
  Russia 84, 89
  Slovakia 131
Meiji restoration 64
mental illness, Russia 81
Menuhin, Yehudi 193
Michnik, Adam 175
middle class
  markets, role of 42

Poland 163, 164, 180, 182
  structural changes 55
  Ukraine 98, 103
migration 29
  from and to Croatia 113
  within Poland 168
military
  Croatia 118
  Poland 170
Milosević, Slobodan 189
mixed economies 28
models 22–3, 185–93
Moldova 81, 82, 86
money supply
  Russia 91
  Ukraine 97–8
monopolies
  markets, role of 42
  Russia 90
  Ukraine 108
morality
  Commonwealth of Independent States 91–3
  Croatia 113, 121, 123
  Hungary 157
  Poland 168, 173
  Russia 81, 85
Moslems 61
Mosse, W.E. 64
Movement for a Democratic Slovakia 130, 134
Movement for Poland's Reconstruction (ROP) 175, 176, 177, 178
Multilateral Investment Guarantee Agreement (MIGA) 59n.15

Naisbitt, John 44
Napoleonic civil code 148
National Alliance of Trade Unions (Poland) 165, 169
National Bank of Slovakia 128–9
National Council of the Slovak Republic 130
National Democrats (Poland) 174
nationalism 38, 39, 49, 54
  Commonwealth of Independent States 87
National Labour Bureau (Slovakia) 138